Winter Treats
and
Summer Delights

TO JACK, HARRY AND GRACE

With love, Mummy

Winter Treats
and
Summer Delights

FERN BRITTON
AND
SUSIE MAGASINER

ANDRE DEUTSCH

ACKNOWLEDGEMENTS

My thanks to Susie for all her expert cooking knowledge.
Without her, this book would never have happened.
Thank you, too, to Mummy, Lauren, Sue and Sheila,
who not only look after me, the children and the house,
but also had to taste some experiments that *didn't* work!
And all my love and thanks to Phil, who has given me such encouragement
and support in the last few months, and for feeding me
potato waffles and fried eggs at midnight!

First published in Great Britain in 1999 by André Deutsch Ltd
76 Dean Street
London W1V 5HA

www.vci.co.uk

Copyright © Fern Britton and Susie Magasiner 1999

The rights of Fern Britton and Susie Magasiner to be identified as the authors
of this work have been asserted by them in accordance with the
Copyright, Designs and Patents Act 1988

A catalogue record for this book is available from the British Library

ISBN: 0 233 99557 9

Photography: Michael Michaels
Food preparation: Susie Magasiner and Helen Bernard
Styling: Maria Kelly
Illustrations: Vivien Rothwell
Design: Rob Kelland

Printed in the UK by Butler and Tanner, Frome and London

2 4 6 8 10 9 7 5 3 1

Contents

Introduction

Susie and I first thought of the idea of winter and summer food as we sat out in my back garden on a warm spring day. We thought of all the truly delicious fresh produce available in summer and the favourite things we liked to eat. The idea of winter food followed quite naturally. We imagined the comfort of drawing the curtains at 5.00 pm. Sitting by the fire hearing the wind howling round the chimney. And the smell of something gorgeous in the oven. So that's when we decided to bring our favourite recipes for summer and winter together, in Winter Treats and Summer Delights.

I do hope that you enjoy cooking and eating the food in this book. Here's to good results for you and full tummies all round!

Love

Fern

Winter Menus

*T*hese are a collection of recipes that work well together. Read the tip boxes on the recipes to see how you can get ahead. Remember cooking for friends and family is as much about the people as the food, so don't be over ambitious. You don't have to serve three courses but you may want to serve vegetables or a salad. Entertaining is not an exam: first and foremost you should enjoy the cooking, the eating and the company.

THREE WINTER WARMING MENUS FOR ENTERTAINING:
Broccoli and potato soup *page 17*
Beef and pearl barley stew with dumplings *page 35*
(serve with green vegetable)
Rhubarb toffee pudding *page 65*

Minestrone soup *page 14*
Venison casserole with chestnuts *page 37*
(serve with mashed potatoes)
Marmalade orange steamed pudding *page 64*

Honeyed duck breasts *page 30*
Apple relish *page 30*
Braised red cabbage with apples *page 51*
(serve with green beans and potatoes)
Chocolate and cherry roulade *page 62*

FAMILY SUPPER:
Easy chicken and tomato curry *page 25*
Cinnamon rice pilaff *page 53*
Baked pears *page 57*

SUNDAY LUNCH:
Rustic chicken liver pâté *page 18*
Roast pork and crackling with apricot
        and pistachio stuffing *page 40*
Chilli roast potatoes *page 53*
Carrot and swede mash *page 52*
Baked apples *page 57*

DINNER FOR FRIENDS:
Butter bean and roast garlic soup *page 16*
Moroccan lamb stew with prunes *page 32*
(serve with couscous or mashed potatoes)
Apple meringue pie *page 56*

FISHY DINNER PARTY:
Risotto Parmigiana with peas *page 48*
Baked fillet of trout with a scarlet sauce *page 44*
Potato latkes *page 52*
Green salad
Roasted autumn fruits with vanilla *page 58*

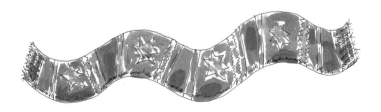

Summer Menus

TWO COLD SUMMER LUNCHES
    TO PREPARE AHEAD OF TIME:
Peperonata *page 78*
Circassian chicken *page 88*
Raw courgette and tomato salad with bulghur *page 80*
Baby leaf spinach salad with Blue Vinnie
    and bacon *page 81*
Yoghurt and orange semolina cake *page 121*

Baba ganoush *page 77*
(served with warm pitta)
Bacon and egg tortilla *page 73*
Raw courgette and tomato salad *page 80*
Tomato and pine nut salad *page 79*
Arranged fruit platter *page 124*

A FISHY MEAL:
Pasta and seafood salad *page 83*
Roast fillet of sea bass with ginger and
    spring onions *page 98*
Warm tomatoes with Boursin *page 111*
Summer fruit mousse *page 124*

A POSH DINNER PARTY OR LUNCH:
Asparagus with balsamic dressing *page 72*
Salmon en croûte with prawn filling *page 100*
Potato salad with mojo mayonnaise *page 85*
Cucumber mint and yoghurt salad *page 83*
Summer fruit terrine *page 123*

TURKISH FARE:
Cheese borek *page 74*
Kofte kebabs with houmous dressing *page 92*
Green beans with bacon and peppers *page 112*
Ricotta, orange and chocolate tart *page 126*

A MEAL FOR A PERFECT SUMMER'S DAY:
Mexican guacamole *page 75*
Seared tuna fillet with warm salade Niçoise *page 97*
Ricotta, orange and chocolate tart *page 126*

A FAMILY SUPPER:
Peppered smoked mackerel pâté *page 76*
Chicken and pasta bake *page 26* or
    Summer stuffed vegetables *page 90*
      (serve with salad)
        Jazzed-up ice cream *page 126*

BBQ PARTY:

Chicken pieces in garlic and rosemary marinade *page 95*

Lamb kebabs in Adobo marinade *page 96*

Mexican guacamole *page 75*

Potato salad with Mojo mayonnaise *page 85*

Raw courgette and tomato salad with bulghur *page 80*

Baby leaf spinach salad with Blue Vinnie
and bacon *page 81*

Hazelnut torte with raspberry and cream filling *page 120*

A CASUAL SUPPER FOR FRIENDS:

Fish and scallop couscous with harissa
and fried pitta *page 102*

Go wild chocolate flan *page 118*

A VEGETARIAN SUPPER FOR FRIENDS:

Spinach and feta pancake stack *page 108*

Tomato and pine nut salad *page 79*

Arranged fruit platter *page 124*

A SUNDAY LUNCH:

Loin of pork in vinegar and paprika marinade *page 96*

Summer dauphinoise *page 110*

Petit pois à la Français *page 113*

Roasted aubergines and tomatoes *page 111*

Any pudding you fancy *pages 116-127*

How to make the recipes work best for you...

SERVINGS:

■ How much each of us eats is a very individual thing and so serving quantities should be taken as a guide line. On the whole, I would like to believe that I have been generous in the quantities suggested, assuming that main meals will probably be accompanied by vegetables.

PREPARATION TIME:

■ As somebody who chops fairly fast and works in a semi-methodical way in my kitchen and knows the recipes like the back of my hand, I am at an unfair advantage here. I also take the shortest method by using a food processor for blending and an electric whisk for whipping egg whites or cream. If you are doing these tasks by hand, then recipes will take longer. All other preparation tasks, such as chopping, peeling, and general tasks you will need to perform before you start cooking, are done by hand and I hope to have given a reasonable indication of the time they will take.

COOKING TIME:

■ This time includes any cooking that may need to be done in a recipe, whether it is in preparation or in completion of the dish. In the lasagne, for example, the various sauces will be included in the cooking time, as will the final baking of the dish, but the assembly of the dish will have been included in preparation time.

■ Note: All eggs are medium sized unless otherwise it is otherwise stated.

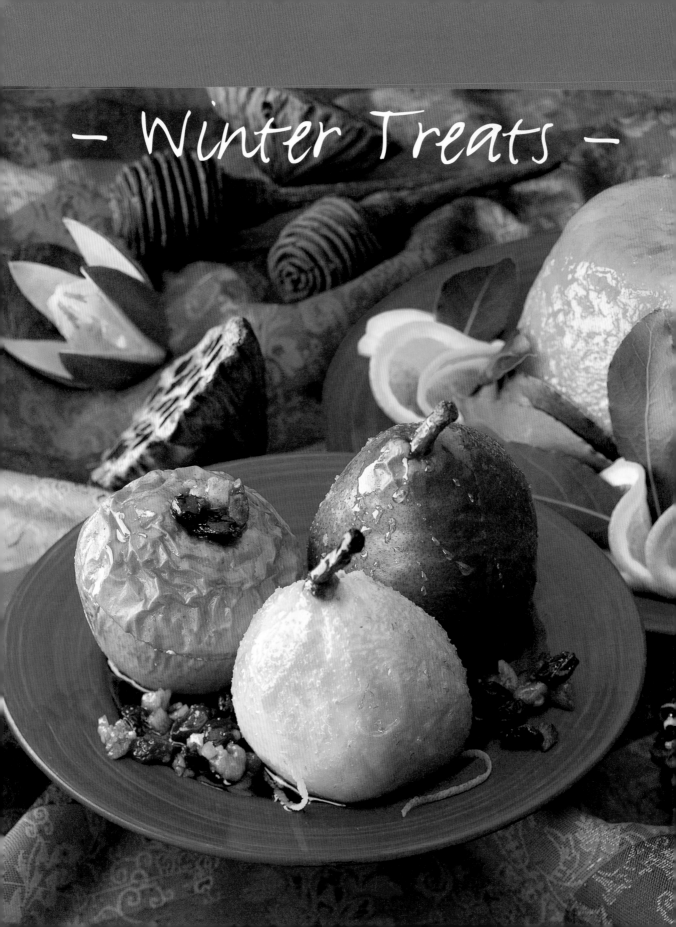

– Winter Treats –

Winter food is obviously very comforting but it can also be very romantic. Susie and I had dreams in our heads of the kind of food we need during the long, cold, dark months. My particular dream was to have a home-made hot pasty in my pocket while out on a long walk with the children. Or a bowl of butter bean and garlic soup with hot butter soaked bread on Bonfire night. And the all-time definitive winter warmer, a pot of beef and barley stew with dumplings on a frosty Sunday night.

We have taken lots of short cuts in these recipes, and have used lots of good convenience food too. I do hope you enjoy cooking, and more importantly, eating your way through this book. I am not one of the world's naturally gifted cooks, but I am a normal mum who has to feed the family, and if I can make something that tastes good anyone can! Good luck and enjoy!

Love

Jenn

Warming casseroles, stews, spices, chillies and chestnuts are what cold winter days call out for. I have included several aromatic, hot one-pot dishes, warming soups and bakes to help us through the long, dark afternoons and plenty of rib-sticking puddings to ward off the cold.

Susie

Soups and Snacks

Left: Minestrone and Thai Chicken Soup

Minestrone

PHOTOGRAPH ON PAGE 12

*S*usie's mother always makes an enormous pot of Minestrone to have in the evening after her New Year's day lunch party. There are inevitably a few people who are in need of reviving! This soup always does the trick. It's not only comforting, but incredibly good for you too. Always use the biggest cooking pot you possess because of the enormous volume of vegetables. When I made this for Phil he was very impressed because, apparently, an authentic Minestrone has so many vegetables in it that you can stand a spoon up in it! This passes the test!

SERVES 4–6 ■ PREPARATION TIME 15 MINUTES ■ COOKING TIME 40 MINUTES

– Ingredients –

3 tbsp olive oil, plus more to serve

125g / 4½ oz cubed pancetta
        or streaky bacon

1 red onion, chopped

250g / 9oz potato, peeled and cut into
        1cm / ½ inch cubes

115g / 4oz celery, diced

225g / 8oz green beans, topped and tailed
        and cut into 2.5cm / 1 inch lengths

225g / 8oz carrots, peeled and diced

400g / 14oz tin chopped tomatoes in tomato
        juice or 300ml / ½ pint bottled
        chopped tomatoes

salt and pepper

400g / 14oz tin canellini beans

85g / 3oz white cabbage, shredded

2–3 tbsp green pesto sauce,
        plus more to serve

freshly grated Parmesan

FERN'S TIPS

■ This soup is even better reheated the following day.

– Method –

■ Heat the oil in a very, very large saucepan. Add the pancetta and cook for 2 minutes. Add the red onion, potato, celery, green beans and carrots and stir. Add the tomatoes, cover generously with water, season with plenty of salt and pepper, then bring to the boil and simmer for 30 minutes.

Add the canellini beans, cabbage and pesto and cook for a further 5 minutes.

To serve, ladle spoonfuls of the soup into large bowls, and garnish with a teaspoon of pesto and a generous sprinkling of Parmesan. An extra drizzle of good quality olive oil and black pepper will finish it off perfectly.

SOUPS AND SNACKS

Thai Chicken Soup

PHOTOGRAPH ON PAGE 12

*T*his soup is a meal in a pot that's more like a stew – but an enormously exotic stew! I adore the fresh Thai flavours of lemongrass, ginger and kaffir lime leaves. Everything about them is fragrant and somehow romantic. And there's no problem in getting hold of them – strong flavoured lime leaves, perfumed lemongrass and ginger are all available in the average supermarket. This recipe is for a subtly flavoured soup with a very mild kick of chilli. If you like strong flavours then by all means add more lemongrass and chilli, or serve with a bottle of chilli sauce for the brave to splash on top. Although my children didn't like the soup, they did like the chicken, rice and vegetables that I took from the soup with a slotted spoon.

SERVES 4–6 AS A MAIN COURSE ■ PREPARATION TIME: 20 MINUTES ■ COOKING TIME: 1 HOUR 10 MINUTES

– Ingredients –

1 stick lemongrass, very finely chopped (you
    may need to remove some of the outer
    leaves if they're a bit old and woody)

2.5cm / 1 inch peeled ginger root, very finely
    chopped

1 large clove garlic, very finely chopped

1–2 mild green chillies, de-seeded and finely
    chopped

1 tbsp vegetable oil

3 carrots, diced

3 sticks celery, diced

1.3kg / 3lb oven-ready chicken

4–5 fresh or dried kaffir lime leaves

1–2 tbsp fish sauce, depending on taste,
    optional

salt and pepper

115g / 4oz long grain rice,
    rinsed through a sieve

175g / 6oz frozen peas

85g / 3oz or more, chestnut or shitake
    mushrooms, sliced

4 tbsp chopped coriander

shop-bought fried shallots or onions
    to garnish, optional

– Method –

■ Make sure that the lemongrass, ginger, garlic and chilli are chopped as finely as possible. Heat the oil in a large saucepan into which the whole chicken will fit with a lid on. Add the finely chopped spices and the carrots and celery, stir and sauté for 3–4 minutes.

Check that the chicken is clean, and remove any excess fat from the cavity. Put into the pot along with the lime leaves, fish sauce, and salt and pepper. Cover with water and a lid and poach over a gentle heat for 45 minutes, then add the rice and cook for a further 15 minutes or until you're sure the chicken is no longer pink.

Remove the chicken and, when cool enough to handle, peel away the skin and remove the meat in bite-sized chunks. Skim the surface of the soup with a spoon to remove the excess fat, then return the chicken to the pan. Add the peas and mushrooms and cook for 10 minutes more. Check the seasoning and then, just before serving, stir in the coriander.

Serve in large bowls, as everyone will want plenty. Scatter a few fried shallots or onions on top if you wish.

Butter Bean and Roast Garlic Soup

*R*ecipes with a very short list of ingredients are right up my street. I hope you think so too! This soup is very quick and very easy, and just the thing after a bracing night carol singing with the Brownies. It's also a rather hip dinner party starter. The only warning I offer is that it's best to eat it with close friends as the garlic is, well, garlicky!

SERVES 4–6 ■ PREPARATION TIME 10 MINUTES ■ COOKING TIME: 35 MINUTES

– Ingredients –

1 whole bulb garlic

olive oil

2 x 400g / 14oz tins butter beans
   or 3 if you want a very thick soup

850ml / 1½ pints vegetable stock

1 sprig rosemary

salt and pepper

– Method –

■ Pre-heat the oven to 220°C / 425°F / gas mark 7.

Take the whole unpeeled bulb of garlic and slice off the top to reveal the individual cloves. Drizzle with a little olive oil, wrap in foil and bake in the oven for 25 minutes until soft.

Rinse the butter beans and drain. Put into a saucepan with the stock and rosemary. When the garlic is cooked and cool enough to handle, squeeze out the purée and add to the soup mixture. Season with salt and pepper and simmer for 5–10 minutes.

Remove the rosemary and liquidize the soup. Check the seasoning and serve.

FERN'S TIPS

■ Add a dollop of Greek yoghurt and a few snipped chives to each bowl when serving.

■ For a more substantial soup, add some sliced frankfurters or crispy bacon to the soup and simmer briefly.

Broccoli and Potato Soup

*A*ctually, I would say this is really a great steaming bowl of broth. It's rustic and chunky and fabulous just on its own with a hunk of fresh French bread and butter. All this and it's good for you!

SERVES 4 ■ PREPARATION TIME 15 MINUTES ■ COOKING TIME 20 MINUTES

– Ingredients –

1 tbsp olive oil

25g / 1oz butter

1 medium leek, quartered lengthways
       and chopped

½ onion, chopped

1 large clove garlic, chopped

225g / 8oz potato, peeled and cut into
       1cm / ½ inch cubes

salt and pepper

700ml / 1¼ pints vegetable or chicken stock

350g / 12oz head broccoli

8 basil leaves

freshly grated Parmesan to serve

– Method –

■ Heat the oil and butter in a large saucepan. Add the leek and onion and cook over a gentle heat until translucent. Add the garlic and potato, season and stir, cooking gently for 2–3 minutes. Add the stock, turn up the heat and simmer for 10 minutes.

Cut off the broccoli florets – you do not want to use much of the stalks – and tear into the smallest florets or roughly chop. Add to the soup and cook for a further 5 minutes. Tear up the basil leaves and stir into the soup. Serve straight away with a sprinkling of Parmesan.

FERN'S TIPS

■ The broccoli stalks can be peeled and sliced and added to stir fries. By all means add them to the soup if you like, at the same time as the potatoes; the soup will just be more rustic.

Rustic Chicken Liver Pâté

*T*here is something very comforting about eating pâté. Particularly when it's spread on thick buttery toast, sluiced down with a glass of warming port or a steaming cup of tea. This Italian-style pâté is very easy and economical, and makes a delicious starter. It will keep well in the fridge for a snack in front of Coronation Street the next day! What more could you ask!

SERVES 6–8 ■ PREPARATION TIME: 12 MINUTES ■ COOKING TIME: 20–25 MINUTES

— Ingredients —

450g / 1lb chicken livers
70g / 2½ oz butter
175g / 6oz onion, finely chopped
2 cloves garlic, crushed
a good splash of brandy
2 tbsp Greek yoghurt
50g / 1¾ oz tin anchovy fillets
2 tsp capers
salt and pepper
fresh bay leaves to garnish

— Method —

■ Wash the chicken livers, trim away any sinews or green parts.

Melt the butter in a frying pan and, when foaming, add the onion and cook for 3 minutes until translucent. Add the garlic (which takes less time to cook than onion, and tastes horrible if it burns) and cook for 1 minute before adding the livers. Cook these for 8 minutes over a gentle heat until they are just cooked through. Just before the end of cooking add a splash of brandy to the pan.

Tip three-quarters of the liver into a food processor, add the yoghurt and purée until smooth. Add the rest of the livers, along with the anchovies and capers, and pulse a few times to chop but not purée. Season with plenty of black pepper and salt to taste, but remember the anchovies are salty too.

Put into a buttered china dish and refrigerate for at least 30 minutes to set. You can cover the pâté with more melted butter (which gives it a wonderful yellow waxy coat) and keep it for three days in the fridge. Decorate the dish with fresh bay leaves.

Cornish Pasties

I have a romantic idea of taking a long wintery walk with the children and stopping to unwrap a warm home-made pasty from my pocket. They are also good eaten with soup or served cold at a picnic on warmer days. Pasties were originally eaten by miners, who could hold onto the pastry seal with dirty hands. They would then eat the rest and throw away the grubby bit.

MAKES 8-9 13CM / 5 INCH PASTIES ■ PREPARATION TIME: 20 MINUTES ■ COOKING TIME: 1 HOUR

— Ingredients —

140g / 5oz lean rump or sirloin steak,
    finely chopped
115g / 4oz potato, cut into small dice
85g / 3oz swede, cut into small dice
¼ medium onion, chopped
a splash of Worcestershire sauce
1 tsp Dijon mustard
a pinch of mixed dried herbs
salt and pepper
500g / 1lb 2oz shortcrust pastry
    (I use ready-made)
1 egg, beaten with a pinch of salt

— Method —

■ Pre-heat the oven to 220°C / 425°F / gas mark 7.

Mix together the steak, potato, swede, onion, Worcestershire sauce, mustard and herbs. Season well with salt and pepper.

On a floured surface, roll out the pastry until it is 5mm / ¼ inch thick. Use a saucer or similar round shape that is approximately 13cm / 5 inches in diameter as a template, and cut out as many circles as you can. Gather the odd shapes of pastry into a ball and re-roll until you have eight or nine circles.

Divide the filling between the circles. Wet the edges of the circles with a little water and press the edges closed to enclose the filling in the pasties. Twist the sealed edge over to secure the seal. Place the pasties on a lightly oiled baking sheet. Brush each pasty liberally with baken egg and bake for 10 minutes. Then turn down the oven to 170°C / 325°F / gas mark 3 and cook for 45-50 minutes more.

SOUPS AND SNACKS

Welsh Rabbit

*C*heese on toast is a favourite snack, especially with tomato soup. Here is the real McCoy. It is thick with cheese and requires a knife and fork rather than fingers! This is a dish that was traditionally served at the end of a meal as a savoury, but it makes a great light meal or snack. The trick is to use a thick slab of white farmhouse-style bread rather than ready sliced.

MAKES 2 SLICES ■ PREPARATION TIME: 10 MINUTES ■ COOKING TIME: 4–5 MINUTES

– Ingredients –

2 slices thick white bread

85g / 3oz grated Cheddar cheese

40g / 1½ oz butter, softened

2 tbsp boiling milk

Worcestershire sauce

cayenne pepper

salt and pepper

– Method –

■ Lightly toast one side of the bread. In a saucepan over low heat, work the cheese and butter to a paste, then add the milk a little at a time, stirring. Season with a few drops of Worcestershire sauce and a pinch of cayenne pepper, taste and add salt and pepper if needed. The seasoning will depend on the strength of cheese you use. Spread the mixture thickly onto the untoasted side of the bread and place in a shallow baking dish. Brown under a hot grill and serve.

FERN'S TIPS

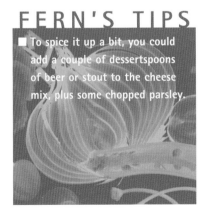

■ To spice it up a bit, you could add a couple of dessertspoons of beer or stout to the cheese mix, plus some chopped parsley.

Main Courses

– Poultry –

25   EASY CHICKEN AND TOMATO CURRY

26   CHICKEN AND PASTA BAKE

27   TURKEY GOUJONS WITH A CRUNCHY HAZELNUT CRUMB

29   WHOLE ROAST DUCK

30   HONEYED DUCK BREASTS WITH APPLE RELISH

– Meat –

32   MOROCCAN LAMB STEW WITH PRUNES

34   LAMB SHANKS BRAISED WITH WINE AND SPICES

35   BEEF AND BARLEY STEW WITH DUMPLINGS

36   STIR-FRIED CHILLI BEEF WITH AUBERGINE AND SWEET POTATO

37   VENISON CASSEROLE WITH CHESTNUTS

38   BOSTON STYLE SAUSAGE AND BEANS WITH CHILLI CORN MUFFINS

40   ROAST PORK AND CRACKLING WITH APRICOT AND PISTACHIO STUFFING

– Fish –

42   FINNAN HADDIE BAKED IN A CREAM SAUCE

43   PRAWN AND CHICKEN JAMBALAYA

44   BAKED FILLET OF TROUT WITH A SCARLET SAUCE

Left: Boston Style Sausage and Beans with Chilli Corn Muffins

Easy Chicken and Tomato Curry

One Saturday morning, I was making this for lunch. The windows were open and the cooking smells soon wafted out to where Phil was washing the car. (I want you to picture our very glamorous life.) He came tearing in, wanting to have a taste and then had the nerve to suggest it needed a couple of spoonfuls of mango chutney just to balance the spices. Unfortunately, he was right. Anyway, I think you'll enjoy playing around with your own blend of curry spices. A food processor makes it very simple to mix. Leave out the chilli if you think a milder version would be more popular in your household.

SERVES 4 ■ PREPARATION TIME 5 MINUTES ■ COOKING TIME 35 MINUTES

– Ingredients –

1 onion, very roughly chopped

1 red pepper, de-seeded and roughly chopped

2 salad tomatoes, quartered

2.5cm / 1 inch piece of ginger root,
    peeled and sliced

3 cloves garlic, sliced

1 chilli, de-seeded, optional

1 tbsp sunflower oil

20g / ¾ oz butter

8 boneless, skinless chicken thighs
    or other cuts of chicken

1–2 tsp turmeric

1–2 tsp cumin

1 tsp salt

150ml / ¼ pint chicken stock,
    you may need a little more

·1 dsp mango chutney

juice of ½ – 1 lemon

fresh chopped coriander leaves to garnish

– Method –

■ Put the onion, red pepper, tomatoes, ginger, garlic and chilli (if using) into a food processor and blend to a smooth paste. If making by hand then chop or grate the ingredients as finely as you can and then crush in a mortar and pestle.

Heat the oil and butter in a large sauté pan and add the chicken pieces. Wait till they loosen from the bottom of the pan before turning over and cook for 5 minutes each side. Add the onion paste to the pan along with the turmeric, cumin and salt. How much of the spices you add will depend on your taste. Stir and cook until the paste has reduced and the mixture almost 'fries' again.

Add the stock, cover the pan and cook gently for 20 minutes. Stir in the mango chutney, squeeze over the lemon juice and sprinkle the coriander on the top before serving.

Serve with cinnamon rice pilaff, page 53, to soak up the delicious sauce.

FERN'S TIPS

■ This curry reheats well, and can be frozen.

WINTER TREATS

Chicken and Pasta Bake

*P*asta bakes are very popular in my family and I like the fact that they give you a clear 25 minutes to do something else - like have a row with the kids – whilst it is in the oven.

SERVES 4 ■ PREPARATION TIME 20 MINUTES ■ COOKING TIME 40 MINUTES

– Ingredients –

350g / 12oz penne

2 tbsp olive oil

1 medium onion, finely chopped

2 cloves garlic, chopped

4 boneless, skinless chicken breasts,
  cut into bite-sized pieces

salt and pepper

125g / 4½ oz chorizo sausage, thinly sliced
  (this is a lovely oily, spicy sausage but
  the skin can be a bit tough so skin it
  first if you prefer)

150g / 5½ oz button or chestnut mushrooms,
  sliced

1 small glass dry white wine

300g / 10½ oz crème fraîche

10–12 basil leaves, finely shredded

1 tbsp chopped parsley

85g / 3oz Fontina cheese, cut into small cubes

85g / 3oz Gruyère, grated

– Method –

■ Pre-heat the oven to 200°C / 400°F / gas mark 6.
  Boil the pasta in plenty of salted water until just al dente, then drain.
  Meanwhile, heat the oil in a large frying pan and fry the onion until soft but not coloured. Add the garlic and chicken and cook for 10 minutes. Season well with salt and pepper.
  Add the chorizo sausage and mushrooms and fry for a couple of minutes, then add the wine and cook for a few more minutes before adding the crème fraîche and herbs.
  Mix the chicken in with the cooked pasta, stir in the cubes of Fontina and check the seasoning. Pile into an ovenproof dish and sprinkle over the Gruyère. Bake in the oven for 25 minutes.

FERN'S TIPS

■ Fontina is a mild soft Italian cheese rather like Port Salut in texture, which you could use instead.

MAIN COURSES: POULTRY

Turkey Goujons
with a crunchy hazelnut crumb

*A*lthough my children still prefer dinosaur-shaped turkey they will eat these and, what's more, grown-ups love them too. The toasted hazelnuts in the crumb crust make them quite special and so much better than shop bought.

SERVES 4 ■ PREPARATION TIME 20 MINUTES ■ COOKING TIME 25–30 MINUTES

– Ingredients –

4 turkey breast steaks

juice of ½ lemon

55g / 2oz wholemeal bread

100g / 3½ oz whole shelled hazelnuts

finely grated rind of 1 lemon

3 tbsp flour

salt and pepper

1 egg, beaten

a drizzle of oil, olive or sunflower

lemon wedges to serve

– Method –

■ Pre-heat the oven to 190°C / 375°F / gas mark 5.

Cut the turkey into 2.5cm / 1 inch strips across the grain and toss in the lemon juice.

Process the bread into fine crumbs and tip into a shallow dish. Toast the hazelnuts in a dry pan over a moderate heat until golden; this will really bring out their flavour, but remember they'll burn the minute your back is turned. Allow them to cool, then put them in the food processor and blend until they are like breadcrumbs. (If you process them when they're too warm, the natural oils are released and you get a horrible sludge.) Then mix with the breadcrumbs and grated lemon rind.

Season the flour with salt and pepper and tip into a shallow dish or plate. Tip the egg into a similar dish. Next dip the pieces of turkey one at a time first into the flour then into the egg and then finally into the crumb mixture, making sure that all of the turkey is evenly covered in crumbs. Lay onto a greased baking tray and repeat until all the pieces are done.

Drizzle olive or sunflower oil over the goujons; if you have a pump spray of oil use that. Bake for 25–30 minutes until the crumb is crunchy and the turkey is cooked. Alternatively you could shallow fry them for 15 minutes, turning them halfway through.

Serve with lemon wedges.

A Bit about Ducks...

*D*omestic rather than wild ducks are available almost year round in the supermarkets, sold fresh and frozen. Butchers and supermarkets may carry a variety of breeds, such as Gresham, Barbary and Norfolk, depending on the season. Oven-ready ducks weigh between 1.3–2.7kg / 3–6lb, and you should allow at least 450g / 1lb per person on the bone.

Cooking a duck is simple. Remove any excess fat from inside the cavity. Pre-heat the oven to 200°C / 400°F / gas mark 6 and roast for 20 minutes per 450g / 1lb plus 20 minutes, then allow to rest for 10 minutes before carving.

Carving is the problem. Unlike a chicken, a duck has a large bone frame and the wing and leg bones are quite thick. If you want to make a really good job of it for a dinner party, you may need to use poultry shears to cut away the legs and wings before you start to carve the breast. This is tricky and can be quite messy.

I must admit I burnt the first duck I roasted, it was black and smoking – but it tasted delicious, the skin especially. The two of us didn't bother to carve it, we picked at it with our fingers in front of the television, and accompanied it with some new potatoes and salad. Greatly recommended.

Anyway, here is a recipe for whole roast duck, as everyone should try the superb flavour of duck roasted on the bone at least once. Next time you may decide to opt for the duck breasts, especially if having them at a dinner party, since you can impress your guests by fanning the breasts onto the plate before serving.

Whole Roast Duck

SERVES 3 ■ PREPARATION TIME 8 MINUTES ■ COOKING TIME 1 HOUR 40 MINUTES

– Ingredients –

1 oven-ready duck weighing at least
    2kg / 4lb 8oz

1 red onion, peeled and quartered

1 lemon, quartered

1 large sprig fresh rosemary

1 large sprig fresh sage

1 tbsp runny honey

1 tbsp soy sauce

1 tbsp Cointreau, brandy or other spirit

– Method –

■ Pre-heat the oven to 200°C / 400°F / gas mark 6.

Remove the giblets and liver from inside the duck, keep the liver to add to the Apple relish recipe on page 30 if you like, but discard the rest. Pour a kettle of boiling hot water over the duck to loosen the fat under the skin. Pat dry and prick the skin several times with a fork.

Stuff the cavity with the onion, lemon and herbs. Place on a roasting rack in a roasting tin and roast for 20 minutes per 450g / 1lb. Halfway through the cooking time, pour off the excess fat and use it to roast potatoes. Twenty minutes before the end of the cooking time remove the duck from the oven. Mix together the honey, soy sauce and Cointreau or other spirit and brush over the bird. Return to the oven and cook for the remaining 20 minutes. Rest for 10 minutes under foil before carving.

Serve with Braised red cabbage with apples (page 51), roast potatoes and most definitely the Apple relish.

MAIN COURSES: POULTRY

Honeyed Duck Breasts
with Apple Relish

*B*uy Barbary duck breasts rather than Aylesbury if you can. They are leaner and plumper.
Apples are the perfect partner for duck, as are spices and dried fruits. This relish combines all such flavours and cuts perfectly through the richness of the meat. It would also be delicious served with roast pork, as an alternative to plain apple sauce, or with sausages or cold ham.

THE DUCK SERVES 4 ■ PREPARATION TIME 5 MINUTES ■ COOKING TIME 25 MINUTES
THE RELISH SERVES 4–6 ■ PREPARATION TIME 10 MINUTES ■ COOKING TIME 15 MINUTES

– Ingredients –

4 duck breasts

2 tbsp runny honey

2 tbsp soy sauce

FOR THE APPLE RELISH

15g / ½ oz butter

1 medium red onion, chopped

225g / 8oz cooking apple, peeled and diced

50ml / 2fl oz strong cider

40g / 1½ oz dried fruit, such as dried sour cherries, cranberries or raisins

¼ tsp ground cinnamon

1 tsp freshly grated ginger root or a pinch of dried ginger

2–3 sage leaves finely chopped or a pinch of dried

1 tbsp runny honey

salt and pepper

FERN'S TIPS

■ Cooking apples turn brown very quickly. To prevent this, squeeze lemon juice over the apple or cover with acidulated water (water and lemon juice mixed).

– Method –

■ Pre-heat the oven to 220°C / 425°F / gas mark 7.

Heat a frying pan large enough to accommodate all the duck breasts without crowding over a high heat and, when hot, add the duck breasts skin side down. You will not need any oil as the fat will come out of the skin. Fry for a few minutes until the breasts are pale gold, then transfer them to a roasting tin and roast in the oven for 12-15 minutes depending on how well cooked you like them.

Remove the breasts from the oven. Mix together the honey and soy sauce and brush onto the breasts. Return to the oven to cook for 5 minutes more.

Allow to rest for 5 minutes before slicing each duck breast into five or six slices, then arrange each one on a plate. Serve with the Apple relish.

Apple Relish

■ Melt the butter and fry the onion until soft. (If you roasted a whole duck and kept the liver, cut it into small pieces and fry along with the onions.)

Add the apple and all the rest of the ingredients and simmer for 8–10 minutes.

The relish can be made ahead of time and reheated, or covered and kept warm for 30-40 minutes before serving.

MAIN COURSES: POULTRY

Moroccan Lamb Stew with Prunes

*T*his really is a wonderful stew to come home to. It's full of enticing flavours and is rich and warming. It doesn't take too long to prepare and, like any stew, tastes better the next day. It freezes well too. To give it an extra exotic dimension we've finished it with orange flower water (available from delicatessens and supermarkets). Use the leanest lamb you can get – the best is from the leg – and ask your butcher to bone and cube the meat for you.

SERVES 4 ■ PREPARATION TIME 15 MINUTES ■ COOKING TIME 1 HOUR 40 MINUTES

– Ingredients –

900g / 2lb lean whole walnut-sized cubes
    of lamb
2 tbsp sunflower oil
25g / 1oz butter
4–5 shallots, chopped
1 tsp cinnamon
1 tsp ground coriander
a good pinch ground allspice
½ tsp salt and black pepper
3 medium-large carrots, cut into large dice
250g / 9oz 'no need to soak' pitted prunes
1 tsp orange flower water

– Method –

■ Check over the lamb and trim off any fatty bits.

Heat the oil and butter in a sauté pan with a lid. Add the lamb and brown on a high heat for about 5 minutes. Add the shallots and, after a couple of minutes, the spices, salt and pepper, then cook for a few minutes more. Add just enough water to come up to the top of the lamb, cover and cook over a gentle heat for 1 hour.

Add the carrots and prunes and cook for a further 30 minutes, by which time the liquid will have turned into a rich sauce. Check the seasoning and stir well. Sprinkle with the orange flower water and serve with rice, couscous or mashed potatoes.

FERN'S TIPS

■ Shallots can be difficult to peel, but soaking them in boiling water for 5 minutes beforehand makes the job much easier.

Lamb Shanks
braised with Wine and Spices

This to me is what winter cooking is all about, a dish that takes hours in a slow oven allowing you time to read the weekend papers, take the dog for a walk and generally relax. The dish will mostly look after itself, whilst filling your kitchen with warm, welcoming smells. When you serve the lamb it will be so tender you could almost eat it with a spoon. Lamb shanks can be bought from your butcher and some supermarkets. You will need an ovenproof casserole with a lid, either earthenware or cast iron.

SERVES 4 ■ PREPARATION TIME 20 MINUTES ■ COOKING TIME 4 HOURS

– Ingredients –

4 lamb shanks

For the marinade:

250ml / 9fl oz red wine

2 tbsp balsamic vinegar

3 tbsp olive oil

2 bay leaves

3 large cloves garlic, bruised but left whole

1 medium onion, chopped

1 cinnamon stick, broken in two

4 whole cloves

2 whole allspice berries (optional)

8 whole black peppercorns

2 tbsp tomato purée

600ml / 1 pint beef or lamb stock
        (a stock cube will do)

good pinch dried oregano

salt and pepper

250g / 9oz peeled shallots or baby onions

1 tbsp chopped parsley

– Method –

■ Place the lamb shanks in a large non-metallic bowl and add the marinade ingredients. Cover and leave for at least two hours, but preferably overnight, in which case keep it in the fridge. Turn the lamb in the marinade from time to time.

Heat the oven to 150°C / 300°F / gas mark 2. Transfer the lamb and marinade to an ovenproof casserole and add the tomato purée, stock, oregano, salt and pepper (do not add too much salt at this stage as the sauce will reduce and the flavours intensify). Cover the casserole and put it into the oven. After 30 minutes, turn the oven down to 140°C / 275°F / gas mark 1 and continue to cook for 3½ hours. Turn the shanks once or twice during cooking.

In the final hour, add the peeled shallots or onions. If there is a lot of liquid left around the lamb, leave off the lid and turn the heat back up to 150°C / 300°F / gas mark 2 in order to reduce it. Alternatively, at the end of cooking, remove the lamb shanks to a warmed serving dish, skim the surface fat from the sauce and boil to reduce the remaining liquid on the stove. Pour the thickened sauce over the lamb and sprinkle on the parsley before serving.

Beef and Barley Stew
with Dumplings

*T*he definitive winter warmer. A delicious stew thickened by the pearl barley and dumplings. As it is a one-pot meal, you need only serve a green vegetable to go with it. It is very easy to make and requires little fussing over as it cooks. You can even cook it a day or two ahead of time to let the flavours develop, but only make the dumplings on the day you intend to eat it.

SERVES 6 ■ PREPARATION TIME 15–20 MINUTES ■ COOKING TIME 1 HOUR 50 MINUTES

– Ingredients –

85g / 3oz pearl barley

1 tbsp oil

25g / 1oz butter

1 onion, chopped

2 sticks celery, diced

3 carrots, sliced

900g / 2lb lean cubed stewing beef or chuck
 steak, which is very tender

1 tbsp fresh thyme or 1 tsp dried

500ml / 18fl oz stout

300ml / ½ pint beef stock

2 tsp Dijon mustard

Worcestershire sauce to taste

salt and pepper

FOR THE DUMPLINGS:

225g / 8oz self-raising flour

115g / 4oz suet (I prefer vegetable suet)

salt and pepper

1 tsp chopped fresh thyme leaves
 or a pinch of dried

– Method –

■ Pre-heat the oven to 180°C / 350°F / gas mark 4.
Rinse the pearl barley in cold water. Place in a small saucepan, cover with cold water and simmer for 10 minutes, then drain.

Meanwhile heat the oil and butter in a large heatproof casserole and fry the onion and celery until soft but not coloured. Add the rest of the ingredients, including the pearl barley, and season well with salt and pepper. Cover, and cook in the oven for 1 hour.

To make the dumplings, mix all the ingredients together and add just enough water to bind the mixture into a stiff dough. With floured hands, divide the mixture into six balls. Flatten slightly and place on top of the stew. Return uncovered to the oven to cook for a further 30–40 minutes until the dumplings are golden and slightly risen.

MAIN COURSES: MEAT

Stir-fried Chilli Beef
with Aubergine and Sweet Potato

I *always order this in Chinese restaurants. I love both the texture and the heat of the chillies sliding down to warm the tum. I hope you'll enjoy this variation on a theme. It's a good recipe to knock up after you get in from work. It won't take you long. Serve it with frozen microwave rice to be super fast.*

SERVES 4 ■ PREPARATION TIME 15 MINUTES ■ COOKING TIME 15–20 MINUTES

– Ingredients –

1 large clove garlic, finely chopped

2 red chillies, seeded and finely chopped

350g / 12oz rump steak, cut across the grain
    into thin strips

2 tbsp sunflower oil

1 aubergine approx. 225g / 8oz, cubed

225g / 8oz sweet potato, cubed

2 tbsp fish sauce

1 tsp sugar

salt and pepper

small handful fresh coriander leaves, chopped

– Method –

■ Mix the garlic, chillies and steak together and marinade for at least 10 minutes, preferably 30.

Heat the oil in a wok or large pan over a high heat and stir fry the steak. Once browned, add the aubergine and sweet potato. Stir frequently and cook until the vegetables begin to soften, for around 10 minutes. Add the fish sauce and sugar and cook for a couple of minutes. Check the seasoning, adding salt and pepper to taste, stir in the coriander and serve with plain boiled rice.

A bit about Venison...

V *enison comes from red, fallow or roe deer and has the taste and texture of a kind of gamey beef. A wide variety of cuts are available. Loin, saddle and leg are suitable for roasting or braising. Tenderloin chops and steaks are cut from the boned loin and are good flash fried like steak or grilled. The shoulder, neck and breast, which are diced for stewing and are available in sealed packets from the supermarket, are the cuts suitable for this. As venison can be a little dry, it is best marinaded or served with a sauce.*

MAIN COURSES: MEAT

Venison Casserole with Chestnuts

T his I would say, is one of the great festive dishes. Tomorrow you have a lorry load of relatives arriving and tonight all you have to do is put another log on the fire, wrap a few presents and pop some venison into its marinade. Once the meat is steeped overnight, tomorrow's cooking is half done! (Please don't be put off by the long list of ingredients – enjoy getting everything weighed measured and chopped before you start.) The combination of the rich meat and soft chestnuts is very seductive. And the chestnuts are easy. They come whole, already peeled and cooked in vacuumed packs or tins. Serve with great dollops of buttery mash.

SERVES 6 ■ PREPARATION TIME: 30 MINUTES ■ COOKING TIME: 1 HOUR 15 MINUTES

– Ingredients –

FOR THE MARINADE:

juice and rind of an orange

5 cardamom pods, cracked

1 mace blade or ½ tsp ground nutmeg

4 whole cloves

1 cinnamon stick

4 juniper berries, pricked with a pin

150ml / ¼ pint red wine

700g / 1lb 9oz cubed venison

2 tbsp sunflower oil

1 medium onion, chopped

1 large clove garlic, chopped

2 celery sticks, finely chopped

2 carrots, finely diced

4 rashers rindless, smoked streaky bacon,
*   optional*

4 tbsp brandy

a good pinch dried thyme

300ml / ½ pint beef stock

1 tbsp each tomato purée, soy sauce, and
*   Dijon mustard*

140g / 5oz baby button mushrooms, trimmed

200g / 7oz vacuum packed whole chestnuts

15g / ½ oz plain flour

15g / ½ oz softened butter

– Method –

■ Mix the marinade ingredients together in a large non-metallic bowl. Trim any sinew or fat from the venison. (I have been generous with the weight of meat as this cut can need a lot of trimming.) Stir the venison into the marinade and leave for at least an hour, but overnight, covered, in the fridge is best.

Take the meat from the marinade, removing any cloves or cardamom, and reserve the liquid. Pat the meat dry with absorbent paper.

Heat 1 tbsp of the oil in a casserole, add the onion, garlic, celery, carrots and bacon, and cook until the onion is translucent, then tip onto a plate.

Wipe out the casserole. Turn up the heat, add the remaining oil and, when hot, add the venison and brown. Quite a lot of liquid will come out of the meat. After 4–5 minutes it will be cooking in its own gravy. Add the brandy and thyme and return the sautéed vegetables. Strain the marinade juices and add along with the stock, tomato purée, soy sauce and mustard. Add salt and freshly ground black pepper to taste.

Cover and cook either over a gentle heat on top of the stove or in an oven pre-heated to 190°C / 375°F / gas mark 5 for 40 minutes.

Add the mushrooms and chestnuts and cook for a further 15 minutes. Mix the flour and butter into a smooth paste and stir into the casserole, bring to the boil and cook on top of the stove for 5 minutes more, stirring from time to time until the sauce thickens.

MAIN COURSES: MEAT

Boston-style Sausage and Beans
with Chilli Corn Muffins

PHOTOGRAPH ON PAGE 22

*T*his is a real winter warmer, a dish to keep the cowboys warm around the camp fire. The beans have a slightly sweet-sour tang to them and can be spiced up with chilli sauce. Use your favourite kind of sausage – I like the garlic Toulouse variety – but any good meaty sausage will do. Serve the corn muffins warm, with or without butter, like a roll. This casserole is good made the day before and reheated but the muffins are best straight from the oven.

SERVES 6 ■ PREPARATION TIME 15 MINUTES ■ COOKING TIME 35 MINUTES

– Ingredients –

8 good meaty sausages

2 tbsp sunflower oil

1 red onion, chopped

2 sticks celery, sliced

2.5cm / 1 inch cube fresh ginger root,
    peeled and coarsly grated

1 clove garlic, chopped, optional

400g / 14oz tinned chopped tomatoes

1 tbsp tomato purée

400g / 14oz tin mixed pulses,
    rinsed and drained

400g / 14oz tin canellini beans,
    rinsed and drained

1 tbsp whole grain mustard

1 tbsp soft brown sugar

1/8 tsp ground allspice

1/2 –1 tsp chilli sauce

115g / 4oz button mushrooms, quartered

salt

chopped parsley to garnish

– Method –

■ Small sausages look really good but are not essential to the dish. To make them, gently squeeze the middle of a sausage and carefully twist, then divide with a sharp knife or scissors. Heat 1 tbsp of the oil in a frying pan and cook the sausages until browned all over.

Meanwhile heat the rest of the oil in a large saucepan and fry the onion until soft. Add the celery, ginger and garlic (I wouldn't add the latter if using a garlic sausage, but otherwise it is a good idea), and cook for a few minutes before adding the rest of the ingredients.

Cook for at least 25 minutes, stirring occasionally, then add the sausages. Sprinkle with parsley and serve with the muffins.

Chilli Corn Muffins

MAKES 12 LARGE MUFFINS ■ PREPARATION TIME 10 MINUTES ■ COOKING TIME 25 MINUTES

– Ingredients –

2 eggs

225ml / 8fl oz buttermilk

½ tsp chilli power or 1 tsp chilli sauce

115g / 4oz butter, melted

175g / 6oz tin sweetcorn, drained

25g / 1oz freshly grated Parmesan

140g / 5oz self-raising flour

140g / 5oz cornmeal

1 tbsp baking powder

½ tsp salt

a good pinch of dried thyme

– Method –

■ Pre-heat the oven to 200°C / 400°F / gas mark 6.

Break the eggs into a large bowl, add the buttermilk, chilli and melted butter and whisk. Stir in the sweetcorn and Parmesan. Mix the remaining ingredients together and add to those in the bowl, gently them in until combined. Spoon into greased muffin tins, filling them almost to the top as the mixture doesn't rise much. Bake for 25 minutes until golden.

The muffins are best eaten warm and can be made in advance and reheated.

FERN'S TIPS

■ These muffins are good as an alternative to bread rolls with soups or salads or on a picnic.

■ They freeze well too. Try making them in mini muffin tins and serve with drinks as a nibble.

MAIN COURSES: MEAT

Roast Pork and Crackling
with Apricot and Pistachio Stuffing

*R*oast pork and crackling must be one of the all-time great family comfort foods. To get a good crisp crackling, it's important not to baste the meat during cooking. The best cut to use is loin. It is leaner than the
leg and remains quite moist. Get your butcher to score the skin for you or you'll have problems carving later. We
have used a packet stuffing mix as a base for the pistachio and apricot flavours. No one will notice, I bet!

SERVES 4–6 ■ PREPARATION TIME 20 MINUTES ■ COOKING TIME 2 HOURS

– Ingredients –

1.3 kg / 3lb rolled loin of pork with skin

1 tbsp oil

1 tsp salt

85g / 3oz sage and onion stuffing mix

250ml / 9fl oz boiling water

55g / 2oz pistachio nuts, roughly chopped

85g / 3oz dried apricots, chopped

grated rind of a lemon

freshly ground black pepper

– Method –

■ Pre-heat the oven to 190°C / 375°F / gas mark 5.

Score the skin of the pork if the butcher hasn't already done so. Place
the pork on a rack in a roasting tray, rub the skin with the oil and salt, and
roast for 30 minutes per 450g / 1lb, plus 30 minutes (the weight I have
suggested will take 2 hours to cook). When it comes out of the oven, leave
to rest for 10 minutes under foil to keep it warm. (I have invested in a
meat thermometer which removes the guesswork. It's brilliant. It has a long
probe which you stick into the meat at the start of cooking. On the dial it
has pictures of whatever meat you're cooking and when it gets to the
animal you want, it's cooked!)

To make the stuffing, add the boiling water to the sage and onion
stuffing mix, then stir in the remaining ingredients. Shape into six large
balls and add them to the roasting tray 25 minutes before the end of
cooking.

For ease of carving it is best to remove the crackling and cut it up
separately before bringing the joint to the table.

MAIN COURSES: MEAT

WINTER TREATS

Finnan Haddie baked in a Cream Sauce

Susie's American grandfather was, unusually for those times, the cook in the family and this is one of the dishes he loved to make. It is comforting and rich. Serve it with rice or baked potatoes.

SERVES 4 ■ PREPARATION TIME 10 MINUTES ■ COOKING TIME 35 MINUTES

– Ingredients –

700g / 1lb 9oz undyed smoked haddock
    fillets, skinned
40g / 1½ oz butter
1 mild onion, chopped
40g / 1½ oz plain flour
125ml / 4fl oz dry white wine
175ml / 6fl oz double cream
a little salt
pepper
6 plum tomatoes, sliced
chopped parsley to garnish

– Method –

■ Pre-heat the oven to 180°C / 350°F / gas mark 4.

Divide the haddock into four pieces, put into a pan of cold water over a high heat. Bring to the boil, then drain - the fish only needs to be heated through. This will stop the haddock being too salty or strongly flavoured.

Melt the butter in a saucepan and cook the onion until soft but not coloured, add the flour and stir until blended. Gradually add the wine and the cream, stirring continuously. Let it cook for a couple of minutes and season, but only add a little salt as smoked haddock is quite a salty fish.

Place the fish in an ovenproof dish, pour over the sauce and layer the tomatoes on top. Bake for 20 minutes and sprinkle with chopped parsley just before serving.

SUSIE'S TIPS

■ You can turn this into a macaroni bake, by flaking the partly-cooked fish, mixing it with the sauce and some cooked macaroni, and topping it with a layer of tomatoes and some grated Cheddar.

Prawn and Chicken Jambalaya

*J*ambalaya is from the Southern state of New Orleans in the USA. It usually consists of chicken and rice, although I have broken with tradition and added prawns and chorizo, a spicy salami-style sausage too. My version is probably more a combination of paella and jambalaya, but whatever it is, it is a great informal, one-pot meal and it won't matter if you keep it warm in an oven for half an hour if you don't want to rush everyone to the table. If you don't like prawns then add a little more chicken instead and vice versa.

SERVES 4 ■ PREPARATION TIME 20 MINUTES ■ COOKING TIME 40 MINUTES

– Ingredients –

2 tbsp olive oil

1 onion, chopped

1 red pepper, quartered and sliced

1 green pepper, quartered and sliced

2 sticks celery, sliced

2 boneless skinless chicken breasts,
    cut into bite-sized pieces

salt and pepper

115g / 4oz chorizo sausage, sliced

175g / 6oz easy cook long grain rice

2 tsp paprika

1–2 cloves garlic, crushed

1 tsp chilli sauce

600ml / 1 pint chicken stock

2 tbsp tomato purée

1 bay leaf

225g / 8oz large peeled prawns

4 spring onions, finely sliced

– Method –

■ Heat the oil in a large sauté pan with a lid. Fry the onion until soft then add the peppers and celery and cook for 3–4 minutes before adding the chicken, salt and pepper. When the chicken has cooked on the outside, add the sausage and rice and stir to ensure that the grains are covered in the oil.

Add the paprika, garlic and chilli sauce and cook for 1 minute before adding the stock, tomato purée and bay leaf. Stir and bring to the boil, then lower the heat, cover, and leave to cook gently for 20 minutes. After this time check the seasoning and add the prawns and spring onions and cook for a further 5 minutes making sure that the prawns have heated right through.

Serve garnished with a few finely chopped green ends of spring onion sprinkled on top.

Baked Fillet of Trout
with a Scarlet Sauce

*T*he fish is wrapped in greaseproof paper to seal in flavour, then baked in a hot oven. Although I have suggested using trout you could use haddock, cod, or halibut if you prefer, but remember to ask your fishmonger to skin it for you. The vivid scarlet colour of the sauce is from beetroot, flavoured as the Scandinavians would with caraway and fennel seeds. I like to serve this with potato latkes (page 52).

SERVES 4 ■ PREPARATION TIME 15 MINUTES ■ COOKING TIME 20 MINUTES

– Ingredients –

4 trout fillets weighing 175g / 6oz each,
    skinned
4 bay leaves
2 tbsp olive oil
salt and pepper
1 red onion, chopped
1 clove garlic, chopped
400g / 14oz tin chopped tomatoes in tomato
    juice or bottled tomato sugo
½ tsp fennel seeds
½ tsp caraway seeds
4 small cooked beetroot in vinegar,
    fresh not bottled, finely chopped
    or coarsely grated
1½ tsp sugar
sprigs of dill to garnish

– Method –

■ Pre-heat the oven to 200°C / 400°F / gas mark 6.
    Line a baking tray with greaseproof paper or foil, leaving plenty of overhang. Place the fish fillets on top and put a bay leaf on each. Drizzle with a little of the oil (use about half) and season with salt and pepper. Fold up the edges and crimp to close. Bake in the oven for 10-12 minutes. Take out and leave to rest for a couple of minutes.
    Meanwhile heat the remaining oil in a saucepan, adding more if necessary, and fry the onion. When soft, add the garlic, and cook briefly before adding the tomatoes, fennel, caraway, salt and pepper. Cook for 10 minutes over a moderate heat until the tomato has thickened. Add the beetroot and sugar and cook for a few minutes more to warm it through.
    Serve the fish, minus the bay leaf, with some of the sauce and a sprig of dill to garnish.

WINTER TREATS

Vegetarian and Vegetables

Left: Risotto Parmigiana with Peas, and Ratatouille with Polenta

Risotto Parmigiana with Peas

PHOTOGRAPH ON PAGE 46

*T*his risotto is made from ingredients you could easily keep in your store cupboard, all except the Parmesan, which should be bought fresh, although a lump will last ages in the fridge. The combination of flavours may sound a little unorthodox but, trust me, they are made for each other. Next time you are shopping, buy the ingredients (making sure you get tinned petit pois, as they are sweeter and smaller than ordinary peas) and make this when you open the fridge and think there is nothing to eat.

SERVES 4 ■ PREPARATION TIME 5 MINUTES ■ COOKING TIME 20–25 MINUTES

– Ingredients –

2 tbsp olive oil

1 onion or 4 shallots, finely chopped

350g / 12oz risotto rice

1 litre / 1¾ pints hot vegetable stock

3 tbsp light soy sauce

400g / 14oz tin petit pois, drained and rinsed

55g / 2oz butter, diced

8 tbsp freshly grated Parmesan

a pinch of ground nutmeg

– Method –

■ Heat the oil in a large saucepan and gently fry the onion or shallots until soft. Add the rice, stir to coat each grain in the oil, and cook for a couple of minutes until the edges of the rice begin to turn translucent. Keep the stock hot, ideally simmering in a saucepan, and add enough to the rice to stop the pan hissing. Stir the rice slowly as it absorbs the liquid, then add more stock, repeating the process until all the stock has been used. The risotto should be creamy not dry. Add the remaining ingredients and stir until the butter and cheese have melted. Serve straight away.

Ratatouille with Polenta

PHOTOGRAPH ON PAGE 46

*R*atatouille contains all my favourite Mediterranean vegetables – aubergines, courgettes, tomatoes, onions and green peppers. Sadly, however, it is often served as a watery, flavourless dish. I make mine in a wok over a fairly high heat to ensure that the tomatoes reduce, resulting in a thick rich dish. Served with polenta, it makes a substantial vegetarian meal.

SERVES 4 ■ PREPARATION TIME 15 MINUTES ■ COOKING TIME 20 MINUTES

— Ingredients —

FOR THE RATATOUILLE:

3 tbsp olive oil

1 large clove garlic

1 large mild onion, diced

225g / 8oz aubergines, diced

225g / 8oz courgettes, sliced

1 large green pepper, and 1 large red pepper,
    quartered and thickly sliced

400g / 14oz tin Italian tomatoes

salt and pepper

2 tbsp tomato purée

½ tsp dried thyme

1 tsp dried oregano

FOR THE POLENTA:

600ml / 1 pint vegetable stock

85g / 3oz polenta

3–4 tbsp freshly grated Parmesan

a knob of butter

— Method —

■ Heat the oil in a wok or large saucepan, large enough to take all the vegetables. Bash the garlic with the flat side of a knife, add to the oil and fry briefly before fishing out and discarding (this will just add a mild hint of garlic to the dish). Add the onion and then the other vegetables, except the tomatoes, and stir fry for 5 minutes until all the vegetables start to soften. Season them with salt and pepper and add the tomatoes, tomato purée, thyme and oregano. Turn up the heat and cook, stirring from time to time, until the tomatoes bubble fast and reduce to a fairly dry mixture. Check the seasoning.

Meanwhile make the polenta by bringing the stock to the boil in a saucepan. Add the polenta slowly in a steady stream, stirring continuously, and cook for 2–3 minutes until it is the consistency of soft mashed potato. Take off the heat and stir in the Parmesan and butter. Season well with salt and freshly ground black pepper.

Serve the polenta on plates with the ratatouille spooned on top.

FERN'S TIPS

■ Ratatouille tastes even better reheated the next day. It can also be eaten cold. Don't forget it is a great vegetable dish to serve with any grilled or roast fish and meat.

VEGETARIAN AND VEGETABLES

Lasagne Verdi
with Spinach and Ricotta

*L*asagne is a real family favourite, however do not embark on making one if time is short – all lasagne needs two sauces, plus time in the oven to bake. I am as fond of vegetarian lasagne as I am of that made with meat, although sometimes vegetarian lasagne can be a bit bland and if you've been through the process of making one, it's got to be worth it. Here I have combined spinach, broccoli, pesto and Parmesan for good flavour.

SERVES 6 ■ PREPARATION TIME 40 MINUTES ■ COOKING TIME 50–60 MINUTES

– Ingredients –

800g / 1lb 12oz fresh spinach leaves
        or 450g / 1lb frozen leaf spinach
2 tbsp olive oil
1 large onion, chopped
1 large leek, washed well and thinly sliced
1 bulb fennel, chopped
200g / 7oz broccoli, broken into small florets
        or purple sprouting broccoli
salt and pepper
1½ tbsp pesto sauce
375g / 13oz lasagne
250g / 9oz ricotta
55g / 2oz pine nuts, toasted in a dry pan
55g / 2oz shavings of Parmesan
25g / 1oz freshly grated Parmesan

FOR THE BECHAMEL SAUCE:

55g / 2oz butter
55g / 2oz plain flour
850ml / 1½ pints milk
salt and pepper
a good pinch of freshly grated nutmeg

– Method –

■ Pre-heat the oven to 180°C / 350°F / gas mark 4.

If using fresh spinach, wash it well, remove any tough stalks and cook in just the water clinging to the leaves in a very large pan. You may need to cook it in two batches. If using frozen, simply defrost. Either way, drain the spinach, leaving it in a colander weighed down by a plate with a couple of tins on top (you can leave it overnight if you like). Alternatively, when cool enough, you can squeeze the spinach in your hands. It should be fairly well drained but not 'dry'. Chop the spinach and set to one side.

To make the filling, heat the oil in a large pan, add the onion, leek and fennel and fry until soft. Then add the chopped spinach and broccoli. Season well and cook over a gentle heat for 5 minutes then add the pesto.

To make the béchamel sauce, melt the butter in a large saucepan, add the flour, stir to a paste and cook gently for a minute. Add the milk in a steady stream, whisking continuously. Simmer gently for 5 minutes until the sauce is thick and glossy. Season with salt, pepper and nutmeg.

To assemble the lasagne, oil a large ovenproof dish. Put a layer of the pasta on the bottom and cover with a thin covering of béchamel, then some of the vegetables. Dot with some of the ricotta, and sprinkle over some of the pine nuts and Parmesan shavings. Add another layer of pasta, spoon on more of the béchamel and repeat the process. You should have three layers of vegetables, each dotted with ricotta, pine nuts and Parmesan. The top layer should just be pasta generously covered in béchamel. Scatter grated Parmesan on top and bake in the oven for 50–60 minutes until the pasta is cooked and the top is golden and bubbling.

VEGETARIAN AND VEGETABLES

Braised Red Cabbage with Apples

*T*his is my favourite way to cook red cabbage. It is delicious with duck, pork or other rich meats and tastes even better made in advance and reheated the next day.

SERVES 4–6 ■ PREPARATION TIME 15 MINUTES ■ COOKING TIME 1 HOUR

— Ingredients —

1 medium sized red cabbage
    approx. 650g / 1lb 7oz
1 tbsp cooking oil
1 medium sized onion, chopped
1 cooking apple, diced
salt and pepper
2 tbsp cider vinegar
1 tbsp soft brown sugar
pinch each of cloves and allspice
25g / 1oz butter

— Method —

■ Pre-heat the oven to 170°C / 325°F / gas mark 3 (or cook on top of the stove).

Remove any wilted outer leaves and cut the cabbage into 2.5cm / 1 inch wedges, removing the heavy core, and then slice them across. Rinse under cold water – a bright blue colour will come out of it.

Heat the oil in an ovenproof casserole and gently fry the onion for a couple of minutes. Add the cabbage and the apple and turn until all have been coated in the oil. Season generously, add the vinegar, brown sugar, spices and a tablespoon or two of water. Put on the lid and cook gently on the top of the stove or in the oven for 45–50 minutes. Check that the cabbage isn't drying up about halfway through and, if necessary, add a little more water.

Stir in the butter before serving to add a richness and gloss to the dish.

Carrot and Swede Mash

*B*oth carrots and swede have an innate sweetness that goes really well with roast meat. I love mashes, be they potato, broad bean, or parsnip, they are comforting and good to eat.

SERVES 4–6 ■ PREPARATION TIME 8 MINUTES ■ COOKING TIME 15 MINUTES

– Ingredients –

350g / 12oz carrots
350g / 12oz swede
25g / 1oz butter
salt and black pepper

– Method –

■ Peel and cut the carrot and swede into 2.5cm / 1 inch chunks. Boil in salted water until tender. Drain and mash together with a potato masher. Work in the butter and season well.

Potato Latkes

PHOTOGRAPH ON PAGE 45

*T*hese are fried potato cakes that are a bit like a rosti. They are a staple part of Jewish cooking and can be made with a variety of flavours. I like them with the addition of some finely sliced onion.

SERVES 4 ■ PREPARATION TIME 12 MINUTES ■ COOKING TIME 15–20 MINUTES

– Ingredients –

2 large baking potatoes,
    peeled and coarsely grated
1 small mild onion, halved and finely sliced
1 egg, beaten
salt and pepper
3 tbsp plain flour
½ tsp baking powder
oil for frying

– Method –

■ Mix all the ingredients together. Heat a little oil in a frying pan and drop spoonfuls of the mixture into the pan. Flatten a little and cook over a gentle heat so that the potato cooks through without burning. When the underside is golden turn over and cook the other side. You can keep them warm in the oven as you cook another batch. Serve immediately.

Chilli Roast Potatoes

*T*ry these instead of your usual roast potatoes. They are as spicy as you wish to make them!
I think they are addictive, so be warned.

SERVES 6 ■ PREPARATION TIME 15 MINUTES ■ COOKING TIME 1 HOUR

– Ingredients –

1kg / 2lb 4oz potatoes, peeled and cut into
   halves or quarters
   (depending on their size)
1 tsp salt, plus extra for salting the potato
   water
1½ –2 tbsp chilli sauce
4 tbsp vegetable oil

– Method –

■ Pre-heat the oven to 190°C / 375°F / gas mark 5.
   Put the potatoes into a pan of cold salted water, bring to the boil and
simmer for 6 minutes. Drain thoroughly and swirl them around in the
colander to roughen up the surface.
   Mix the salt with the chilli sauce and coat the potatoes with it
thoroughly. Leave for 10 minutes to allow the flavours to develop.
   Heat the oil in a roasting tin, turn the potatoes in the oil and roast for
50–60 minutes until cooked through and golden brown.

Cinnamon Rice Pilaff

*T*hese days I am eating more and more rice, and making a pilaff is a welcome change from just boiling it.
Serve it with stews, casseroles, grills and roasts.

SERVES 4-6 ■ PREPARATION TIME 5 MINUTES ■ COOKING TIME 20 MINUTES

– Ingredients –

1 mug approx 225g / 8oz easy cook long grain
   rice
1 tbsp sunflower oil
15g / ½ oz butter
1 onion, finely chopped
a pinch of ground cinnamon
salt and pepper
1 tbsp tomato purée
2 mugs boiling water

– Method –

■ Measure the rice in a mug, then rinse it in a sieve and drain. Heat the
oil and butter in a large saucepan and gently fry the onion until soft. Add
the rice and stir well so that each grain of rice is coated in oil. Stir in the
cinnamon, season well with salt and pepper, then add the tomato purée.
   Using the same mug you used to measure the rice, add two mugs of
boiling water. Stir, cover, and leave to simmer for 15–20 minutes, until the
water has been absorbed.

VEGETARIAN AND VEGETABLES

WINTER TREATS

Puddings and Baking

Left: Gingerbread Men, Chocolate Fudge Brownies, Grandma's Apple Sauce Teacake

Apple Meringue Pie

*T*he autumn means a wonderful fresh crop of British apples hit the greengrocers. If you've got an apple tree at home, better still! Here are a few really good recipes to make the most of your harvest. There's nothing like the satisfaction of turning your own produce into good grub. This is a variation on lemon meringue pie with a slightly sharp, creamy apple filling and a crunchy meringue topping. It is delicious eaten warm or cold. The recipe requires a tin of condensed milk that needs to be chilled for several hours (overnight is best) in the fridge to thicken before starting the recipe.

SERVES 6–8 ■ PREPARATION TIME 20 MINUTES ■ COOKING TIME 30 MINUTES

– Ingredients –

400g / 14oz tin condensed milk

450g / 1lb dessert apples, peeled and chopped

200g / 7oz packet rich tea biscuits

115g / 4oz melted butter

2 eggs, separated

juice and grated rind of a lemon

115g / 4oz caster sugar

– Method –

■ Put the condensed milk in the fridge to cool for at least an hour, ideally overnight.

Pre-heat the oven to 190°C / 375°F / gas mark 5.

Heat the apples in a pan with a splash of water and cook until soft and pulpy, then leave to cool, beating occasionally to speed up the cooling process.

Crush the biscuits. Use a little of the melted butter to brush a 24cm / 9½ inch ovenproof dish. Add the remaining butter to the biscuits. Reserve two heaped tbsp of the biscuit mixture and use the rest to cover the bottom of the dish and pat down.

Mix together the condensed milk, egg yolks, apple sauce, lemon juice and rind, and pour onto the biscuit base.

Whisk the egg whites until doubled in volume, but not dry and grainy. Whisk in the sugar, a little at a time until you have a glossy meringue. Spoon it over the apple and sprinkle the reserved biscuit crumbs on top. They will give a delicious crunch to the finished pudding. Bake for 25 minutes until golden. Cool a little before serving.

PUDDINGS AND BAKING

Baked Apples and Pears

PHOTOGRAPH ON PAGES 10 - 11

*P*lease don't pooh-pooh the idea of old-fashioned nursery grub. I hadn't eaten baked apples for ages before I made these, and I had forgotten how good they are. And baked pears are a revelation. They're even easier to make than the apples – but look posh enough for dinner parties. Tell everyone that you've gone for minimalist simplicity. Someone is bound to tell you it's good feng shui!

SERVES 4 ■ PREPARATION TIME 5–8 MINUTES ■ COOKING TIME 40 MINUTES

– Ingredients –

FOR BAKED APPLES

4 medium eating apples (e.g. Cox's)

25g / 1oz walnuts, chopped

55g / 2oz raisins

1 tbsp mixed peel, chopped

25g / 1oz soft brown sugar

½ tsp ground cinnamon

a pinch ground cloves

15g / ½ oz butter

FOR BAKED PEARS

8 small pears, (e.g. conference or William)
    allow 2 per person

85g / 3oz sugar

juice and grated rind of an orange

juice and grated rind of a lime

a couple of dried bay leaves

40ml / 1½ fl oz orange flavoured liqueur
    (Cointreau or Grand Marnier)

FERN'S TIPS

■ Try experimenting with the flavours in the stuffing. Use almonds or hazelnuts or even chopped chestnuts. You can add dates, apricots or prunes too.

– Method for baked apples –

■ Pre-heat the oven to 200°C / 400°F / gas mark 6.

Core the apples, wipe the skin and make a shallow cut in the skin of each apple around its circumference. Stand the apples in a baking dish.

Mix together all the remaining ingredients, except the butter, and use to fill the cored apples. Use a teaspoon to pack the mixture down. Dot the top of each apple with a little of the butter. Add 5mm / ¼ inch of water to the bottom of the dish and bake in the middle of the oven for 40 minutes. If the apples are large they may require a few minutes longer.

Serve with plenty of warm custard and golden syrup.

– Method for baked pears –

■ Pre-heat the oven to 180°C / 350°F / gas mark 4.

Either peel or don't peel the pears depending on your preference, but leave the stalk intact. Stand the pears in a baking dish into which they just fit, keeping each other upright. Add all the remaining ingredients except the liqueur and add enough water to come one-eighth of the way up the pears. Bake for 35–40 minutes, basting occasionally. The pears should not wrinkle up but should be just tender. Transfer to a serving dish, pour over the liqueur and basting juices.

Serve hot or cold with a great dollop of clotted cream.

PUDDINGS AND BAKING

Roasted Autumn Fruits with Vanilla

S usie had this brilliant idea. You know how vegetables always taste wonderfully intense after roasting? Well, she thought she'd experiment with fruit to see if there'd be similar results. I'm glad she did as the results are really good and so easy. Served on a large glass plate, covered in their wild plum red syrup with the vanilla pods as a garnish, this looks very pretty and is particularly good accompanied by best vanilla ice cream.

SERVES 6 ■ PREPARATION TIME 10 MINUTES ■ COOKING TIME 15–20 MINUTES

– Ingredients –

85g / 3oz granulated sugar

juice of an orange

1 vanilla pod

6 dark red plums, each cut into 6 segments

5 fresh figs, quartered

2 apples, cored and each divided into 8

2 firm but ripe pears, cored and each
     divided into 8

A small bunch of seedless grapes, left whole

– Method –

■ Pre-heat the oven to 220°C / 425°F / gas mark 7.

First make a syrup by bringing the sugar and orange juice gently to the boil in a pan. Cut the vanilla pod in half lengthways and scrape out the sticky black seeds and add these to the syrup. Boil rapidly for 3 minutes.

Arrange the fruits on a large ovenproof dish. Be careful of metal ones because the fruit acid may react. Pour over the syrup, add the vanilla pod halves and roast for 15 minutes.

Arrange the fruits in a serving dish, pour over the syrup and garnish with the vanilla pods. Serve warm or cold.

PUDDINGS AND BAKING

Grandma's Apple Sauce Teacake

PHOTOGRAPH ON PAGE 54

*T*his recipe comes from Susie's American grandmother and is great for using up windfall apples.
It is baked in a loaf tin and is delicious served sliced at tea time, plain or spread with a little butter.
It is also good for harvest festival or Christmas fairs. Once cooled, the cake can be well wrapped
and it will keep for a couple of days.

PREPARATION TIME 20 MINUTES ■ COOKING TIME 1 HOUR

– Ingredients –

450g / 1lb cooking apples

25g / 1oz granulated sugar

115g / 4oz unsalted butter or margarine

175g / 6oz caster sugar

1 egg, beaten

300g / 10½ oz plain flour

¼ tsp salt

1 tsp baking powder

½ tsp baking soda

1 tsp cinnamon

½ tsp allspice

½ tsp nutmeg

¼ tsp ground cloves

175g / 6½ oz raisins

100g / 3½ oz walnuts, chopped

– Method –

■ Pre-heat the oven to 180°C / 350°F / gas mark 4.

First you need to make a sauce from the apples. Peel, core and chop the apples and put them in a pan with the granulated sugar and a small splash of water. Heat gently for approximately 10 minutes until the apples are softened. (I like it when the apple sauce still has a few lumps, as it adds character to the finished cake.) Remove from the heat and allow to cool.

Cream the butter and caster sugar together until pale and fluffy, then add the beaten egg. Sift the dry ingredients into the wet, then fold in the raisins and walnuts. Spoon into a greased and floured 900g / 2lb loaf tin or a cake tin measuring 23 x 13 x 7.5cm / 9 x 5 x 3 inches or 20 x 20 x 7.5cm / 8 x 8 x 3 inches.

Bake for 50 minutes and allow to cool (ideally turning the cake out of the tin) before serving. If you like, you can make simple icing by mixing icing sugar with a little water and lemon juice, and drizzling it onto the cooled cake.

FERN'S TIPS

■ Make double the quantity of apple sauce and freeze half for next time.
■ You could use toasted chopped hazelnuts instead of walnuts.

PUDDINGS AND BAKING

Chocolate Fudge Brownies

*J*ust the smell of these cooking can make you put on the pounds. They are intensely chocolatey with melted chunks of chocolate in the middle. Look out for American-style plain chocolate chunks in your supermarket as they are larger than chocolate chips, otherwise use chocolate chips or chop a bar of good quality plain chocolate yourself.

MAKES 9 LARGE BROWNIES ■ PREPARATION TIME 10 MINUTES ■ COOKING TIME 30 MINUTES

– Ingredients –

55g / 2oz cocoa powder

50ml / 2 fl oz boiling water

85g / 3oz unsalted butter or margarine,
    melted

225g / 8oz caster sugar

1 egg

½ tsp vanilla essence

100g / 3½ oz plain flour

¼ tsp baking powder

100g / 3½ oz plain chocolate chunks

– Method –

■ Pre-heat the oven to 180°C / 350°F / gas mark 4. Grease a 20cm / 8 inch square cake tin.

Mix together the cocoa, boiling water and half the melted butter and stir well. Add the sugar, egg, vanilla and remaining butter, then sieve in the plain flour and baking powder, and mix well. Stir in the chocolate chunks. The mixture will be fudge-like and shiny. Spread it into the tin and bake for 25–30 minutes. The top should be firm and the cake set. Cut into squares with a sharp knife whilst still warm and leave to cool in the tin.

FERN'S TIPS

■ You can vary the mixture by adding 25g / 1oz mini marshmallows or 55g / 2oz chopped walnuts.

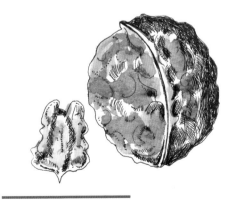

PUDDINGS AND BAKING

Chocolate and Cherry Roulade

*T*his all-time favourite dessert is a very posh Swiss roll. It makes a sophisticated and festive end to
a dinner party. Here I have suggested a cherry and cream filling. The cherries can be soaked in Kirsch
(a strong liqueur made from cherries) or brandy. Do buy good quality chocolate, look for a brand with at least
50% cocoa solids, it makes all the difference. The roulade (the sponge bit of the Swiss roll) needs to cool in
the tin for eight hours after cooking, so this recipe is best started the day before you plan to serve it.

SERVES 8 ■ PREPARATION TIME 30 MINUTES ■ 20 MINUTES, PLUS 8 HOURS' COOLING TIME

– Ingredients –

175g / 6oz plain dark chocolate

2 tbsp water

5 eggs, separated

175g / 6oz caster sugar

For the filling:

450g / 14oz pitted morello cherries
       from a jar or tin

2 tbsp Kirsch

175ml / 6fl oz whipping cream

2 tsp caster or icing sugar

icing sugar to dust

whipped cream, chocolate flakes or curls
       to decorate

– Method –

■ Pre-heat the oven to 190°C / 375°F / gas mark 5.

Line the bottom and sides of a 33 x 23cm / 13 x 9 inch Swiss roll tin
with baking parchment. Melt the chocolate and water together over a
gentle heat then take off the heat to cool a little. Whisk the egg yolks and
sugar together until thick, pale and mousse-like (this can take 10 minutes
by hand or 2–3 minutes using an electric whisk). Gently fold in the
chocolate.

With a clean, dry whisk, beat the egg whites until stiff, then fold into
the chocolate mixture. Pour into the prepared tin and smooth to the edges.
Bake for 15 to 20 minutes. The surface will have risen and will have a
crust. Gently press the centre to make sure it is cooked – if it is cooked, it'll
feel firm. If it isn't, your finger will go straight through the mixture.
Remove from the oven, cover with a sheet of baking parchment and a tea
towel, and leave to cool in the tin for at least 8 hours.

Uncover the roulade and gently spray or sprinkle the crusty surface
with a little water. Lay the baking parchment onto the tea towel, carefully
invert the roulade onto this and peel away the lining paper. Trim the edges
of the roulade using a sharp knife.

To make the filling: drain the cherries and soak in the Kirsch (ideally
during the time the roulade is cooling). Whip the cream until thick,
sweeten with the sugar, then add the cherries and just a little of the Kirsch.
Spread the roulade with the cream and roll lengthways, using the
parchment to help you. It is the nature of a roulade to crack, so don't
panic. Carefully lift onto a plate and dust with icing sugar. You can
decorate with whipped cream or chocolate flakes or curls if you wish.

PUDDINGS AND BAKING

WINTER TREATS

Steamed Orange and Marmalade Pudding

PHOTOGRAPH ON PAGES 10-11

There is something so appealing about a steamed pudding. This one is heavenly – it has a whole cooked orange added to it to make it really moist and delicious. Here are some tips on how to make a good steamed pud:

■ *Get the water ready first, either in a steamer or large saucepan. If using a saucepan, place an old saucer upside down on the bottom to prevent the bottom of the pudding burning.*

■ *Grease your pudding bowl and the greaseproof paper lid well and do not fill more than three-quarters full with pudding.*

■ *To help lift the pudding out of the water, make a long strip of foil and place it under the pudding basin with the foil ends reaching over the sides of the cooking pot.*

■ *Never let the pan boil dry – the water should come halfway up the pudding basin – and top up with boiling water when necessary.*

SERVES 6 ■ PREPARATION TIME: 30–40 MINUTES, INCLUDING COOKING THE ORANGE ■ COOKING TIME 1½ HOURS

– Ingredients –

1 whole orange

115g / 4oz fresh white breadcrumbs

115g / 4oz self-raising flour

1 tsp baking powder

115g / 4oz soft brown sugar

115g / 4oz suet (I prefer vegetable suet)

a pinch of salt

2 eggs, lightly beaten

a little milk

4 tbsp fine cut marmalade

you will also need: a 1.2 litre / 2 pint pudding
    basin, a sheet of greaseproof paper
    and kitchen foil, string or a large
    rubber band

– Method –

■ Place the orange in a pan full of water and boil for 30–40 minutes until the orange is soft.

Mix all of the dry ingredients together in a large bowl. Either purée the cooked orange in a food processor, or chop very finely, collecting the juice and add the whole thing, including the skin and pith but minus the pips. Add the eggs and a little milk until the mixture just drops from a spoon.

Grease the pudding basin with butter or margarine and put the marmalade in the bottom. Pour in the pudding mixture. To cover, lay the greased greaseproof paper on top of the foil and fold a pleat into the centre of both, place on top of the pudding basin and secure with string or a rubber band. Trim any untidy edges and lower into the hot steamer. Keep covered and steam for 1½ hours, checking the water levels now and again.

When cooked, turn the pudding out onto a serving dish. Serve with custard, cream or vanilla ice cream.

PUDDINGS AND BAKING

Rhubarb Toffee Pudding

This is a good old-fashioned family pud, perfect after a Sunday lunch. The rhubarb gets all sweet and sticky at the bottom of the dish. Very delicious, especially with custard, cream or ice cream.

SERVES 4 ■ PREPARATION TIME 15 MINUTES ■ COOKING TIME 40 MINUTES

– Ingredients –

140g / 5oz unsalted butter, softened

55g / 2oz soft brown sugar

250g / 9oz rhubarb

85g / 3oz caster sugar

1 egg

140g / 5oz self-raising flour

4 balls stem ginger, chopped

2–3 tbsp milk

– Method –

■ Pre-heat the oven to 180°C / 350°F / gas mark 4.

Take 55g / 2oz of the butter, cream it together with the brown sugar and use this to cover the bottom of a 1 litre / 1¾ pint ovenproof dish.

Slice the rhubarb 3mm / 1¾ inch thick and scatter on top.

Make the sponge either by hand or in a food processor by creaming the remaining butter and the caster sugar, then add the egg, flour and chopped stem ginger, plus a little milk until the mixture is of dropping consistency. Carefully cover all the rhubarb.

Place the dish on a baking tray to catch any juices that may bubble up over the sides. Bake for 40 minutes. Test that the sponge is cooked, and, if not, return to the oven for a further 5 minutes.

FERN'S TIPS

■ Ginger is especially good with rhubarb. If you cannot get stem ginger you can add 1 tsp of ground ginger along with the flour.

Gingerbread Men

PHOTOGRAPH ON PAGE 54

*J*ust now and again we all get the parental urge to bake with the children. It doesn't usually last too long but when that feeling grips you, these are very satisfying biscuits to make. They're excellent for birthday parties and school fairs, where they always go down well. We have used gingerbread men cutters because we happen to have them! But try Christmas trees, animals, whatever.

MAKES 10–12 BISCUITS ■ PREPARATION TIME: 30 MINUTES PLUS 30 MINUTES RESTING TIME
COOKING AND DECORATING TIME: 20 MINUTES

– Ingredients –

175g / 6oz butter or margarine

175g / 6oz light muscovado sugar

2 eggs, beaten

450g / 1lb plain flour

2 tsp baking powder

2 tbsp ground ginger

2 tsp mixed spice

To decorate:

chocolate drops

Smarties or similar

You will also need a shaped cutter about
9–10cm / 3½ –4 inches long

– Method –

■ Cream the butter and sugar until light and fluffy. Gradually beat in the eggs, then sift in the flour, baking powder and spices and stir until combined. You can make this in a food processor, but take care not to overblend the mixture.

Turn the dough out onto a lightly floured surface and knead until smooth. Wrap in cling film and refrigerate for at least 30 minutes before rolling out.

Heat the oven to 180°C / 350°F / gas mark 4. Roll out the dough on a well floured surface or on non-stick baking parchment if you have some, until the dough is 3mm / ⅛ inch thick. Cut out the gingerbread men and lay them on a lightly greased baking sheet. Re-roll the dough and cut out more gingerbread men until the dough is used up. Bake for 12–15 minutes until pale golden.

Whilst still hot, apply the chocolate drops as eyes and buttons. The heat will melt the chocolate drops and this will act as a fixative. Place Smarties onto the buttons, but leave the eyes plain. Carefully transfer to a cool place until the chocolate has set. (If my kitchen is warm, the chocolate drops can take a while to set and I end up putting them in the fridge.)

– Summer Delights –

Summer food is all about fresh food that is not just salad, salad, salad! It's about eating light, delicious meals that make you feel as if the sun is shining ... even when the heavens are opening!

The food we've made here hopefully fits the bill. How does this sound: asparagus with balsamic dressing, roast sea bass with ginger and spring onions, and summer fruit terrine?

Susie and I are not into fiddling about in the kitchen when we could be out in the sun, so the majority of these recipes are really super quick and easy, I promise.

Have a wonderful summer and may you enjoy every mouthful.

Love

Jenn
x

I really enjoy the informality that summer eating can bring – eating outside, firing up a barbecue or having a picnic. My favourite recipes reflect this and I have included a large number of interesting starters and salads that can be served either individually or three or four dishes at a time, like tapas for a light meal. Friends and family can pass the food around the table and help themselves. The food is bright and colourful with good flavours using seasonal ingredients.

Try the different marinades and enliven vegetables. Lastly, indulge in the best summer puddings ever.

Susie

Starters and Salads

Left: Asparagus with Balsamic Dressing

Asparagus with Balsamic Dressing

PHOTOGRAPH ON PAGE 70

*A*s I don't have a fancy asparagus pan, I can suggest two alternative ways of cooking the asparagus. First, by boiling it in a pan that is large enough to lie the asparagus down in, secondly, by chargrilling it in a ribbed pan until tender.

SERVES 4 AS A STARTER, 2 AS A LIGHT MEAL ■ PREPARATION TIME 5 MINUTES ■ COOKING TIME 5–10 MINUTES

– Ingredients –

450g / 1lb asparagus

salt and pepper

55g / 2oz butter

1 clove garlic, crushed, optional

2 tbsp balsamic vinegar

plenty of Parmesan shavings

– Method –

■ Wash and prepare the asparagus by snapping the tough stalk end – if you bend the end of the stalk, it will naturally break at the point of tenderness. Either boil, covered in a pan of salted water for 5–8 minutes, or heat some oil in a griddle pan and chargrill for approximately 5 minutes. You'll need to test to see if the stalks are tender as the amount of time needed will depend on the thickness of the asparagus.

Lift the asparagus out of the water (or off the griddle pan) with tongs so as not to damage the tips, arrange on serving plates and season with salt and pepper.

Melt the butter in a small pan and add the garlic and cook for 30 seconds. Add the vinegar and stir. Pour over the asparagus and garnish generously with Parmesan shavings.

FERN'S TIPS

■ Make Parmesan shavings by running a vegetable peeler along the sides of a wedge of Parmesan. Some supermarkets sell ready-made fresh shavings in a pot.

Bacon and Egg Tortilla

A tortilla is a wonderful thick firm omelette packed with flavour. Cut it into triangular wedges and serve with ketchup for breakfast, salad for lunch, chips for supper. It travels very easily and can be eaten hot or cold, so it's excellent for picnics. Here is one idea, but add any ingredients you really like.

SERVES 4 ■ PREPARATION TIME 12 MINUTES ■ COOKING TIME 20 MINUTES

– Ingredients –

3–4 tbsp olive oil

1 large onion, chopped

85g / 3oz rindless streaky bacon, finely sliced

225g / 8oz potato, finely diced

salt and pepper

6 eggs, beaten

25g / 1oz finely grated mature
    Cheddar cheese

1–2 tbsp chopped parsley

– Method –

■ If you have a non-stick frying pan that can also go under a grill then use it. If not, don't worry, your omelette will be just as good, but you will need to turn it over.

Heat the oil and fry the onion and bacon until soft. Then add the potato, turn in the oil and cook gently for 10 minutes. Season generously with salt and pepper.

Mix the eggs, cheese and parsley together and add to the pan. Gently stir the mixture with a wooden spoon until the egg starts to firm up, but do not turn it into scrambled eggs! If you have a heatproof pan, transfer to the grill and brown the top of the omelette. Otherwise turn it over by taking a large plate and placing it face down on top of the pan. Tip over and invert the omelette onto the plate then slide the omelette back into the pan to cook the other side for a couple of minutes. Either way leave the omelette to 'set' for a few minutes before cutting into wedges to serve.

FERN'S TIPS

■ Cooked leftover new potatoes work very well in this recipe.

■ You can use sliced leftover cooked sausages or Spanish chorizo (a spicy salami-style sausage).

■ You can make a vegetarian tortilla by adding sliced mushrooms and peppers or courgettes along with the potatoes.

Cheese Borek

PHOTOGRAPH ON PAGES 68-69

These hot cheese parcels are eaten all over Turkey and they have become our favourite nibble to accompany a cold beer before lunch. In Turkey they are deep fried, which you may choose to do if you have a deep fat fryer. If not, bake them in the oven as I do. Do not unwrap the filo pastry until the last minute as it dries out quickly and becomes too crumbly to work with. Keeping it covered with a tea towel or cling film will keep it fresh.

SERVES 4 AS A STARTER (MAKES APPROX. 12 BOREK) ▪ PREPARATION TIME 12 MINUTES ▪ COOKING TIME 15–20 MINUTES

– Ingredients –

250g / 9oz feta cheese

125g / 4½ oz cottage cheese

1 egg

200g / 7oz filo pastry

55g / 2oz melted butter

– Method –

▪ Pre-heat the oven to 200°C / 400°F / gas mark 6.

Break up the feta using a fork and mix to a lumpy paste with the cottage cheese and egg. Do not add salt or pepper, you do not need it.

Cut the filo into strips approx. 7.5cm / 3 inches wide – scissors are best for this. Take one of the strips, lay it out flat and brush it with melted butter. Put a teaspoonful of the cheese mixture onto the bottom left-hand corner of the filo strip. Now here's the fun bit. Fold the bottom left-hand corner over to make a small triangle, now fold that triangle over and so on working your way up the pastry strip. You will end up with a neat triangle filled with cheese. Place on a lightly greased baking sheet and brush with a little more butter. Repeat the process until you have used up all the pastry and filling.

Bake for 15–20 minutes until pale golden. They are best eaten hot or warm.

Fold over any overlapping pastry

Final fold

4th fold

3rd fold

2nd fold

1st fold

FERN'S TIPS

▪ *You can assemble the borek a few hours before you need to bake them.*

▪ *For a variation, try adding ½ tsp of dried mint to the mixture.*

Mexican Guacamole

*S*upermarket guacamole is green and creamy. However in Mexico it is quite different as the ingredients are chopped – not blended – as finely as possible to give it a rougher texture. Popular myth has it that if you keep an avocado pip and bury it in the guacamole, it will help prevent the avocado from discolouring. By all means try this, but it hasn't worked for me. This recipe was given to a friend of Susie's by her Mexican au pair. She serves it as a starter with tortilla chips. It's informal and fun, and the flavours are so clean and good. If you're in the mood to feel really hip, get a few bottles of Mexican beer and stuff wedges of squeezed lime in the bottle necks. Hola!

SERVES 6 AS A STARTER OR 12 AS A DIP ■ PREPARATION TIME: 15–20 MINUTES

– Ingredients –

1 medium red onion

4 plum tomatoes

2–3 mild green chillies, de-seeded

2 avocados

juice of 1½ –2 limes

½ tsp salt

at least 55g / 2oz chopped coriander

– Method –

■ To make the guacamole as delicious as possible, it is necessary to chop the ingredients very finely. It does take a little time but it is worth it. If chopping is really not your thing, then chop the onion, tomatoes and chilli in a food processor and only roughly fork the avocado by hand.

Mix all the ingredients together and serve.

FERN'S TIPS

■ If you buy unripe avocados, place them in a paper bag and put them in a dark place, where they will ripen overnight.

■ By the way, I prefer Hass avocados, the ones with the dark rough skin, as they have a good flavour and peel easily.

Peppered Smoked Mackerel Pâté

Smoked mackerel fillets can be turned into a really delicious pâté. Serve with thin triangles of wholemeal toast or pitta bread cut into soldiers.

SERVES 4–6 ■ PREPARATION TIME 5 MINUTES

– Ingredients –

3 peppered smoked mackerel fillets (approx. 280g / 10oz)

200g / 7oz full or half fat cream cheese

150ml / 5fl oz sour cream

1 tsp Dijon mustard

a little chopped parsley to garnish

– Method –

■ Peel the skin away from the mackerel fillets and break them into chunky pieces. If making the pâté in a food processor simply add the rest of the ingredients and process until well combined but not perfectly smooth – the pâté is more interesting with small pieces of mackerel left in it. If making by hand, mash the mackerel with a fork and stir in the remaining ingredients.

Transfer the pâté to a serving dish, cover and refrigerate for a couple of hours. Sprinkle on the parsley before serving. The pâté will keep for a couple of days in the fridge.

STARTERS AND SALADS

Baba Ganoush

PHOTOGRAPH ON PAGES 68-69

*B*aba ganoush is an aubergine flavoured dip along the lines of taramasalata or houmous. Like houmous, it also has tahini in it. Tahini is a sesame seed paste that is available in most supermarkets and health food shops. By the way, this is one for garlic lovers. Once the aubergine is cooked, just put all the ingredients in the food processor and off you go.

SERVES 4 ■ PREPARATION TIME 10 MINUTES ■ COOKING TIME 40 MINUTES

– Ingredients –

1 large aubergine,
   (look for a taut and shiny skin)
1 large or 2 small cloves of garlic,
   roughly chopped
4 tbsp lemon juice
3 tbsp tahini
3 tbsp plain yoghurt
½ tsp salt
a little chopped parsley and a pinch of
   paprika to garnish

– Method –

■ Pre-heat the oven to 220°C / 425°F / gas mark 7.

Place the whole aubergine on a baking tray and bake for 40 minutes until soft. Leave to cool, then carefully peel away the skin with your fingers. Put the pulpy flesh into the processor and blend with all the other ingredients until very smooth. If making by hand, you can pass the aubergine through a sieve and crush the garlic.

Spread the mixture onto a plate or flat bowl and sprinkle with a little parsley and paprika. Serve with warm pitta bread.

FERN'S TIPS

■ *Next time you light up the barbecue, add a whole aubergine and use it to make baba ganoush. It adds a wonderful smoked flavour to the dish. If you use a charcoal barbecue, you can bury the whole aubergine in the dying embers and cook it that way.*

Peperonata

PHOTOGRAPH ON PAGES 68-69

In the days before Ready Steady Cook *I didn't think I liked peppers. But once I understood that you didn't have to eat them raw and unripe (green peppers are simply unripened sweet red ones), I woke up to how delicious they are.*

This simple, low calorie plate of succulent peppers makes a wonderful first course or a delicious light lunch, served with other salads. Skinning the peppers might sound a bit fiddly but it's worth it to have the flesh melt in your mouth. Serve with a hunk of bread and your favourite cheese.

SERVES 4-6 ■ PREPARATION TIME 15 MINUTES ■ COOKING AND COOLING TIME: 1 HOUR

– Ingredients –

5 peppers, a mixture of red, yellow and
        orange
1 tbsp olive oil
2 tbsp chopped flat leaf parsley
15 capers

– Method –

■ Pre-heat the oven to 220°C / 425°F / gas mark 7.

Rub the peppers with the olive oil, place whole on a baking tray and bake in the pre-heated oven for 45 minutes. When soft, carefully place in a large plastic bag and seal. This will help to loosen the skins and catch all the delicious juices that will make up the dressing.

When cool, take a pepper and peel away the skin with your fingers. Discard the seeds and stalk and put the fleshy parts to one side. It doesn't matter if they look a little ragged at this stage. When you have peeled all the peppers, cut into even-sized thin strips and arrange on a plate. I like to keep the colours in groups. Pour over the juices from the bag. Sprinkle over the parsley and capers, and refrigerate before serving.

Good crusty bread goes well with this.

FERN'S TIPS

■ *This dish can be made a couple of days in advance.*
■ *For a spectacular starter, grill some rounds of goat's cheese and serve on individual plates with some peperonata and pretty salad leaves.*

STARTERS AND SALADS

Tomato and Pine Nut Salad

PHOTOGRAPH ON PAGES 68-69

Home-grown, sweet-smelling, sun-warmed tomatoes are the best thing for this recipe but a good shop bought variety left out in a warm kitchen will work just as well. Although neither Susie or I would normally be seen skinning tomatoes, I'm afraid that we both agree that it does make a difference to the flavour in this instance.

Phil has made me realize that most food tastes best served at room temperature. A salad straight from the fridge is too cold and tastes of nothing – and is too much of a shock if accompanying something warm like a steak. The same goes for food that is too hot. A scalding soup serves only to burn your mouth so that you can't taste the rest of the meal. Anyway, this simple salad needs only a sunny day and a garden to sit in. Enjoy!

SERVES 4-6 ■ PREPARATION TIME 10 MINUTES ■ COOKING TIME 5 MINUTES

– Ingredients –

12 vine ripened or plum tomatoes

55g / 2oz pine nuts

salt and pepper

8 basil leaves

3 tbsp olive oil

1 tbsp fresh lemon juice

– Method –

■ Bring a pan of water to the boil. Score the skin of each tomato and drop no more than three at a time into the boiling water for 30–40 seconds. You will see the skin begin to come away. Fish them out with a slotted spoon and plunge immediately into a bowl of very cold water to stop the tomatoes from cooking.

Toast the pine nuts in a dry pan until golden, then tip onto a plate to cool. Do not leave them to cool in the pan or they will burn. Sprinkle with salt.

Slice the tomatoes, arrange on a plate and sprinkle over the pine nuts. Shred the basil leaves and sprinkle on top. Pour over the olive oil, lemon juice and seasoning. You can refrigerate this salad if making it ahead of time, but do take it out of the fridge at least 30 minutes before serving as tomatoes are never good eaten cold.

Two Raw Courgette and Tomato Salads

Growing courgettes in the garden is great but a bit too rewarding. The damn things keep on producing long after you've run out of things to do with them. They are sweet and delicious eaten raw, and we have truly fallen for this combination of courgettes, onion, celery, lemon and cherry tomatoes. We suggest two ways of serving them. The first uses just vegetables, but the second uses bulghur wheat, a cracked wheat that resembles couscous but is a thousand times nicer. It has a coarse texture and is slightly chewy. Like couscous, it is sold in a form that only needs to be soaked rather than cooked, making it ideal for salads.

SERVES 4–6 ■ PREPARATION TIME 10–15 MINUTES ■ COOKING TIME 20 MINUTES

Basic Raw Courgette and Tomato Salad

– Ingredients –

450g / 1lb courgettes, finely grated
2 sticks of celery
3 plum or 8 cherry tomatoes
4 spring onions, trimmed
juice of a lemon
4–6 tbsp olive oil
½ tsp salt
1 clove of garlic, unpeeled

– Method –

■ Put the courgettes into a large bowl. Cut the celery in half lengthways, finely slice and add to the courgettes.

Finely dice the tomatoes and slice the spring onions; add to the courgette-celery mixture and mix well. Add the lemon juice and olive oil - the amount will depend on your taste. Season with salt and bury the garlic still in its skin into the mixture to marinade. Leave for an hour or so for the flavours to develop. Remove the garlic before serving.

Raw Courgette and Tomato Salad with Bulghur

FERN'S TIPS

■ Freshly chopped parsley or mint makes a good addition to the bulghur salad.

– Method –

■ Make the salad as above and whilst the garlic is marinading, prepare the bulghur. Put 85g / 3oz bulghur wheat into a bowl. Add boiling hot vegetable stock until the bulghur wheat is just covered with liquid. Cover with cling film and leave for 30 minutes until the bulghur wheat has swollen and become soft. Drain away any excess liquid and stir the bulghur into the courgette mixture. Serve.

Baby Leaf Spinach Salad
with Blue Vinney and Bacon

*G*ood salads don't have to consist of a thousand bits and pieces with every vegetable intricately chopped and shredded. Salads like that are delicious (when someone else has made it for you), but take ages to make. This is a simply delicious salad using the classic combination of raw spinach and crispy bacon. The peppery rocket and creamy Blue Vinney cheese are simply the icing on the cake. Eat it as a meal on its own or as a starter or side salad.

SERVES 4 AS A LIGHT MEAL OR 8 AS A STARTER OR SIDE SALAD
PREPARATION TIME 8 MINUTES ▪ COOKING TIME 5 MINUTES

– Ingredients –

10 rashers unsmoked rindless streaky bacon

2 slices white or brown bread

oil for frying

225g / 8oz baby spinach leaves, washed

100g / 3½ oz rocket

140g / 5oz Blue Vinney or Stilton cheese

For the dressing:

4 tbsp olive oil

2 tbsp white wine vinegar

4 tbsp plain yoghurt

1 tsp Dijon mustard

a pinch of sugar

salt and pepper to taste

– Method –

■ Slice the bacon into 1cm / ½ inch strips and cut the bread into 1cm / ½ inch cubes.

Heat enough oil in a small saucepan until it is approx. 5cm / 2 inches deep. Test to see if the oil is hot by adding a crumb of bread. If it starts to sizzle immediately it is ready. Add the bacon pieces and deep fry, stirring gently to separate. Cook for 1–2 minutes until they are golden and crispy, then lift out of the oil with a slotted spoon and drain on kitchen paper. Next fry the cubes of bread in two batches, they will take less than a minute to turn golden so watch them carefully, then drain on kitchen paper and sprinkle with a little salt to help them stay crisp.

Put the salad leaves into a large bowl and crumble the cheese on top.

Mix the dressing ingredients together. Pour over the spinach and rocket and toss. Sprinkle over the bacon and croûtons.

FERN'S TIPS

■ You can make the croûtons ahead of time and keep them in an air-tight container.

■ If you already have vinaigrette mixed up or use ready-made then add the yoghurt to 6 tbsp of dressing and leave out the other ingredients.

Pasta and Seafood Salad

*Y*ou can buy ready-prepared seafood cocktail mixes from fishmongers and supermarkets that contain cooked mussels, prawns and squid, to which I like to add a few larger tiger prawns. Choose an interesting shape of pasta, such as radiatore, which looks like old fashioned radiators, or pasta shells for a fishy theme.

SERVES 6 AS A STARTER, 4–6 AS A LIGHT MEAL OR AS PART OF A SALAD BUFFET
PREPARATION TIME 5 MINUTES ▪ COOKING TIME 15 MINUTES

– Ingredients –

250g / 8oz pasta shapes
200g / 7oz seafood cocktail
125g / 4½ oz tiger prawns
115g / 4oz rocket
2–3 tbsp chopped chives
50ml / 2fl oz freshly squeezed lemon juice
125ml / 4fl oz olive oil
salt and pepper

– Method –

▪ Cook the pasta in plenty of boiling, well salted water until al dente, then drain and leave to cool a little.

Add the seafood cocktail and prawns. Shred the rocket, add along with the chives and mix well.

Whisk together the lemon juice and olive oil, season to taste, pour over the salad and mix. Check seasoning and serve. You can refrigerate this, but it is best served at room temperature.

Cucumber, Mint and Yoghurt Salad

*T*he name says it all. A truly cooling and refreshing salad. It is good with cold meat and is the perfect partner to cold poached salmon.

SERVES 6 ▪ PREPARATION TIME 5 MINUTES

– Ingredients –

1 large cucumber, peeled and finely sliced
     (If you do this by machine or mandolin
     you can achieve paper-thin results)
200g / 7oz Greek yoghurt
1 tbsp each chopped mint and chopped dill
salt and pepper

– Method –

▪ Put the cucumber slices in a seive and press down to squeeze out excess juice. Scoop the cucumber into a ball in your hands to squeeze out more juice. As it is the nature of cucumber to retain water, you will not squeeze out all of it. Mix the remaining ingredients together and stir in the cucumber. Chill until ready to serve.

Green Mojo Dressing

A mojo is pesto-like sauce from Spain. There is a red version, which is very fiery and good to eat with grilled meat, but this gentler green version (made with coriander and garlic) was given to Susie by a Spanish friend from the Canary Islands. It's especially good with vegetables and fish. Once made it can be kept covered in the fridge for a couple of weeks and I'm sure you will find all sorts of ways of using it. It makes a fantastic dressing for new potatoes or grilled fish if you dilute it with olive oil and vinegar to taste.
Try stirring a spoonful undiluted into mashed potatoes which is really yummy.

Traditionally this dish is made in a mortar and pestle so that the flavour of the coriander is bruised rather than chopped. However, the summer is not a time to be chained to the kitchen, so do use a food processor if you have one.

■ PREPARATION TIME 10 MINUTES ■

– Ingredients –

1 large handful coriander leaves
    (at least 20g / ¾ oz)
2 tbsp flat leaf parsley
3 cloves garlic, roughly chopped
½ green chilli, seeds removed
    (or 1 chilli if you like it hot)
140g / 5oz pecorino cheese for preference,
    or Parmesan or mature Cheddar,
    (roughly grated)
2 tsp ground cumin
4 tbsp white wine vinegar
4 tbsp olive oil
salt to taste

– Method –

■ Wash and dry the coriander leaves and parsley. Put all the ingredients into the food processor and blend to a smooth paste. You can now use the mojo straightaway. To keep it for longer, transfer into a jar or non-metallic container with a lid and stir in 2 tbsp more olive oil and vinegar.

Potato Salad with Mojo Mayonnaise

*T**his is a good alternative to traditional potato salad using the mojo dressing.*

SERVES 6-8 ■ PREPARATION TIME 10–15 MINUTES ■ COOKING TIME 15 MINUTES

– Ingredients –

1kg / 2lb 4oz baby new potatoes

4 spring onions

140g / 5oz cucumber, unpeeled

75ml / 2½ fl oz mayonnaise

75ml / 2½ fl oz Greek yoghurt

2 tbsp undiluted mojo dressing, see page 84

chopped chives to garnish

– Method –

■ Wash the potatoes and halve if they are on the large side. Place in a large pan of cold salted water, bring to the boil and cook for 15 minutes or until just tender. Drain and set aside. Meanwhile, finely chop the spring onions and cucumber and set aside. Make the dressing by mixing the mayonnaise, yoghurt and mojo together. Stir in the cucumber and spring onions and fold into the potatoes.

I like to serve this salad warm, but it is also good cold. If you add the dressing to the potatoes whilst they are still warm they will have a better flavour, but the dressing will look melted. Give the salad a good stir before serving to bring back its creamy appearance and garnish with chives.

Main Courses

– Poultry –

– Meat –

– Fish –

Left: Chicken and Tarragon Stroganoff

Circassian Chicken

I love this dish. It's a yummy Middle Eastern version of Coronation Chicken, but instead of mayonnaise the spicy sauce is thickened with ground almonds and walnuts. It is very suitable for a buffet party because you make it in advance, serve it cold and it can be eaten easily with a fork. Susie, who is a purist in these matters, says it is one recipe that really benefits from a good home-made stock. So she has included her chicken stock recipe below, using chicken wings for extra speed. (I admit I used a cube!)

SERVES 8 ■ PREPARATION TIME 20 MINUTES ■ COOKING TIME: 45 MINUTES (INCLUDING MAKING YOUR OWN STOCK)

– Ingredients –

FOR THE STOCK:
4 chicken wings
1 onion, peeled, halved and studded
*   with a clove*
1 carrot, peeled and halved
1 stick of celery, halved
a few parsley stalks
a bay leaf
6 peppercorns
a good pinch of salt

8 boneless, skinless chicken breasts
juice of ½ a lemon
100g / 3½ oz blanched whole almonds
100g / 3½ oz walnuts
2 slices of white bread, made into bread-
*   crumbs*
2 tsp chilli sauce
salt and pepper
ground paprika and coriander leaves
*   to garnish*

– Method –

■ To make the stock: put all the stock ingredients into a large saucepan, cover with water and bring to the boil. Turn down the heat and simmer for 20 minutes. Remove the onion, take out the clove and set aside. Strain the stock and return to the pan. (If you already have some stock, add a quartered onion, bring the stock to the boil, simmer for 20 minutes, then remove the onion and reserve.)

Add the chicken breasts and gently poach for 15 minutes or until cooked through. Carefully lift out the chicken from the stock and, when cool enough to handle, tear into bite-sized pieces. Then squeeze over the lemon.

Toast the almonds in a dry pan until golden (the minute you take your eyes off them they'll burn), then either chop along with the walnuts as finely as you can or blend in a processor until they resemble breadcrumbs (take care not to overprocess). Add a splash of the stock and the reserved cooked onion and blend to a paste. Put the nutty mixture into a clean saucepan over a gentle heat and add more of the stock, a little at a time. The mixture will thicken as it cooks, but should have the consistency of double cream. Season with the chilli sauce and salt and pepper.

Pour the sauce over the chicken and mix well, then refrigerate until 1 hour before serving and allow it to return to room temperature. Pile onto a pretty dish and decorate with a sprinkling of paprika and coriander leaves. A few toasted flaked almonds scattered on top of the dish look good.

Serve with rice or couscous, plus a green salad.

Chicken and Tarragon Stroganoff

PHOTOGRAPH ON PAGE 86

*T*he combination of chicken and tarragon in a creamy sauce is a classic. The aniseed flavour of the tarragon is quite powerful, so don't be tempted to overdo it! For a special family supper (your daughter has finally brought the new boyfriend round!) or an informal dinner party, serve it with papardelle, a very wide flat pasta, if you can find it, or tagliatelle that has been tossed in a little butter.

SERVES 4 ■ PREPARATION TIME 12–15 MINUTES ■ COOKING TIME 20 MINUTES

– Ingredients –

4 chicken breasts, cut into strips

2 tbsp seasoned flour

1 tbsp oil

15g / ½ oz butter

3 shallots, finely diced

150ml / ¼ pint stock

10–14 tarragon leaves

12 baby button mushrooms, halved

150ml / 5fl oz sour cream

2 tsp Dijon mustard

salt and pepper to taste

350g / 12oz papardelle or tagliatelle to serve

– Method –

■ Cut the chicken into 1cm / ½ inch strips. Place in a plastic bag with the seasoned flour. Hold the top closed and shake to coat the pieces. Tip into a sieve and shake off any excess flour.

Heat the oil and butter in a large frying pan and gently cook the chicken pieces until golden. Do not move the chicken around in the pan too much – chicken sticks to the pan at first but loosens itself when sealed. After approximately 5 minutes, turn the chicken, add the shallots and cook for a further 4 minutes.

Add half the stock, the tarragon and mushrooms, and stir, scraping up any sediment from the pan. Let the stock bubble away gently, then add the sour cream and mustard. Add more stock as the dish cooks – you want the sauce to be the consistency of single cream. Season to taste and serve on top of the pasta. A few green beans would go well with this.

Summer Stuffed Vegetables

*S*tuffed vegetables may sound a bit old hat, but once you've made and tasted these you'll understand why we've included them. Brimming with the oriental flavours of chilli, shitake mushrooms, coriander and cashew nuts, they make a wonderful summer meal followed by a green salad. Do look out for some of the more unusual varieties of pepper, such as the long bell-shaped Ramiro, or use a mixture of red and yellow peppers. Obviously leave out the chilli and coriander for a milder version if you think you or the kids would prefer it.

SERVES 4 ■ PREPARATION TIME 15 MINUTES ■ COOKING TIME 40 MINUTES

– Ingredients –

115g / 4oz long grain rice or 350g / 12oz
   cooked

4 medium sized red peppers

2 medium to large courgettes

500g / 1lb 2oz extra lean minced pork

1 large clove garlic, crushed

1 green chilli, de-seeded and finely chopped

6–8 shitake mushrooms, chopped

55g / 2oz unsalted cashew nuts,
   roughly chopped

4 tbsp chopped coriander

salt and pepper

2 tbsp olive oil

– Method –

■ Pre-heat the oven to 180°C / 350°F / gas mark 4.

Cook the rice in a large pan of salted boiling water, drain and run under a cold tap to cool, then set aside to drain.

Cut the tops off the peppers and carefully remove the seeds and white membrane. Shave off a thin slice from the bottom of the peppers to help them stand up, but avoid cutting right through. Halve the courgettes lengthways and scoop out the seeds with a small teaspoon, leaving a channel that can be stuffed.

Mix together all the remaining ingredients, except for the olive oil, but including the rice, and season well with salt and pepper. Stuff the peppers as full as possible, packing the stuffing down, and pile the courgettes as high as you can. Rub the skins of the peppers with olive oil and drizzle a little onto the courgettes.

Place the vegetables in an ovenproof dish and bake for 35–40 minutes.

FERN'S TIPS

■ You can make the stuffing in advance and keep it covered in the fridge for 12 hours. You could stuff the veg in the morning and simply bake them that night. They may need a little extra cooking if they are used straight from the fridge.

Pan-fried Pork Fillet with Marsala

*T*his is a very quick supper dish that is easy to make. Marsala is an Italian medium sweet dessert wine, dark mahogany in colour, that can either be used for cooking or drunk on its own. If you like, you could use a medium sherry instead.

SERVES 4 ■ PREPARATION TIME 10 MINUTES ■ COOKING TIME 15 MINUTES

– Ingredients –

450g / 1lb pork tenderloin fillet
2 tbsp flour, seasoned with salt and pepper
1 tbsp oil
25g / 1oz butter
150g / 5½ oz button mushrooms, sliced
6 tbsp or more of Marsala

– Method –

■ Trim the fat away from the fillet and remove the membrane skin that sometimes covers it. Cut it into slices about 5mm / 1/4 inch thick. Place the flour in a bag, add the pork and shake to cover the meat. Tip into a sieve and shake off all the excess flour.

Heat the oil in a large frying pan, add the butter and, when it stops foaming, add the pork. Fry over a hot heat for 3 minutes. Don't worry if the pork will not fit in one layer, move the fillets around as they cook. Turn the pieces over and add the mushrooms, turning them gently in the oil. Fry until the pork is cooked through – the time this takes will depend on the size of your pan, but it should not exceed 10 minutes.

Add the Marsala and cook for 2 minutes. If you want to add more Marsala, do. Serve straight away.

FERN'S TIPS

■ *Add single cream or crème fraîche to the pan after adding the Marsala for a richer sauce.*

MAIN COURSES: MEAT

Kofte Kebabs with Houmous Dressing

*A*n excuse to get the barbecue out! These kebabs transport me back to a sunny, vine-clad restaurant in Turkey. They are very easy to make and would work just as well under the kitchen grill. The houmous dressing is fresh and tasty. All you need to go with it is couscous or buttered rice and a green salad.

SERVES 4 ■ PREPARATION TIME 15 MINUTES ■ COOKING TIME 20 MINUTES

– Ingredients –

500g / 1lb 2oz lean minced lamb

2 cloves of garlic, crushed

1½ –2 tsp ground cumin

½ tsp cayenne pepper

½ tsp ground coriander

salt and pepper

FOR THE DRESSING:

3 tbsp houmous

3 tbsp plain yoghurt

6 mint leaves, finely chopped

1 tbsp chopped coriander leaves

paprika and lemon wedges to garnish

you will also need wooden or metal skewers

– Method –

■ If you intend to use wooden skewers, soak them in water for at least 30 minutes. This will help prevent them burning during cooking.

Mix the lamb and seasoning together – I find that just getting stuck in with your hands works best. Now here is the fun bit: divide the mixture into eight and roll each into a sausage shape. Thread the skewer up through these and press the lamb onto the skewers. Either grill for 10 minutes each side or barbecue.

To make the dressing, simply mix the houmous with the yoghurt and herbs, and hand around separately. It is delicious on the lamb but also on the rice or couscous. I like to sprinkle the kebabs with a little paprika and a squeeze of fresh lemon juice.

Stuffed Burgers

Go to an American restaurant and you can have your burgers any way you want – with cheese, bacon or chilli on top. These burgers have the filling on the inside. Cut into them and a rich melted ooze of cheese runs out. Great for a barbecue or under a grill.

My children loved these plain, and ate small ones, but grown-ups should have a generous sized burger.

SERVES 4 ■ PREPARATION TIME 10 MINUTES ■ COOKING TIME 10 MINUTES

– Ingredients –

1 egg, beaten

salt and pepper

½ tsp dried mixed herbs

a splash of Worcestershire sauce

450g / 1lb minced beef

55g / 2oz Roquefort cheese, divided into
    4 pieces

a little melted butter or olive oil

– Method –

■ Work the egg, salt and pepper, herbs and Worcestershire sauce into the beef. The best way to do this is by hand, but if you are a little squeamish, use a fork. Divide the mixture into four and shape into patties.

Squash a piece of Roquefort into the middle of a burger and carefully cover with the meat so that the cheese is completely covered and is buried at the centre. The burgers will be slightly on the round side but do keep them as flat as you can without allowing any cheese to poke through.

Brush the burgers with a little melted butter or olive oil and cook under a medium-hot grill or on the barbecue for 8–10 minutes, turning halfway through. The cooking time will vary according to how you like your burgers cooked.

FERN'S TIPS

■ *You can add other flavourings to the meat, such as finely chopped onion, a little mustard or even a squirt of tomato ketchup.*

MAIN COURSES: MEAT

Marinades

*M*arinading fish, meat or poultry is the easiest way to make them tender and taste really good. Make the marinade ahead of time, put it into a non-metallic dish, add whatever you want to cook, cover with cling film and leave it in the fridge for up to two days if you like. I always feel that I have already made supper when I do this. If, however, time is short, it is best to marinade at room temperature for up to two hours, turning occasionally. Even 10 minutes will change an otherwise plain chicken breast into something much tastier.

Marinades work well on all cuts of meat and fish that can be grilled, roasted or barbecued. If you like, you can brush on more marinade during cooking, but remember that it has been in contact with raw food and has to be cooked through.

Garlic and Rosemary Marinade

*T*his marinade evokes memories of Italian summer evenings. Rosemary and garlic are a good combination that goes particularly well with chicken pieces and fish.

– Ingredients –

100ml / 3½ fl oz freshly squeezed lemon juice
2 cloves garlic, crushed
200ml / 7fl oz olive oil
salt and pepper
fresh rosemary sprigs

– Method –

■ Mix together all the marinade ingredients. You can either add the rosemary stalks in their entirety or, if you don't mind a few bits of rosemary on your food, you can strip them. I do the latter, as I think it adds more flavour.

Simply grill, roast or barbecue the chicken or fish on both sides until they are cooked.

Vinegar and Paprika Marinade for Pork

his is another Spanish marinade that is particularly good for pork. The amount of vinegar may concern you, but do not worry: it tastes wonderful when cooked. I like to use a boneless, skinless leg or loin which can be left for up to three days. To ensure that the meat is covered with the marinade, the joint and marinade can be put into a plastic bag which is secured at the top, or left in a tall, narrow container (not metal). If using a bowl, cover with cling film and turn occasionally. You could also use chops or pork fillet and marinade for a couple of hours.

– Ingredients –

250 ml / 9fl oz white wine vinegar

2 large cloves garlic, crushed

2 tbsp paprika

1 tsp dried thyme

1 tsp dried oregano

10 black peppercorns

½ tsp salt

2 bay leaves

– Method –

Mix together all the marinade ingredients and add the meat. Either roast in a pre-heated oven 190°C / 375°F / gas mark 5 for 30 minutes per 450g / 1lb plus 30 minutes or barbecue. It is delicious eaten hot or cold.

Adobo Marinade

his is a Spanish marinade that is good for red meat, such as steaks and kebabs, rabbit pieces and fresh tuna steaks.

– Ingredients –

150ml / 5fl oz white wine vinegar

250ml / 9fl oz olive oil

2 cloves garlic, crushed

1 tsp paprika

1 tsp dried oregano

salt and plenty of black pepper

2 bay leaves

– Method –

Whisk together all the marinade ingredients except the bay leaves. Then add the bay leaves. Turn the meat or tuna steaks in the marinade and leave for at least 30 minutes, then grill, roast or barbecue until cooked. If making kebabs, marinade the meat before threading onto skewers.

Seared Tuna Steak
with warm Salade Niçoise

*F*resh tuna is a dense, dark and firm fish that is often sold as steaks. It has an 'unfishy flavour' and may appeal to people who otherwise turn away from fish. This recipe is my adaptation of a classic salade Niçoise, which would usually use tinned tuna. Fresh tuna turns it into a special lunch or light supper. If you have invested in a ribbed griddle pan, now is your chance to use it, otherwise cook the tuna steaks in any heavy pan.

SERVES 4 ■ PREPARATION TIME 30 MINUTES ■ COOKING TIME 25 MINUTES

– Ingredients –

4 x tuna steaks weighing 175g–200g / 6–7oz
*   each*
juice of a lime
1–2 red chillies, seeded and finely chopped
300g / 10½ oz miniature new potatoes
*   or larger, cut in half*
200g / 7oz green beans, stalk end trimmed
1 small cauliflower approx. 300g / 10½ oz,
*   cut into small florets*
4 plum or vine ripened tomatoes, quartered
12 pitted black olives, halved
FOR THE DRESSING:
55g / 2oz hazelnuts
2 tbsp freshly squeezed lemon juice
5–6 tbsp olive oil
salt and pepper
lemon or lime wedges to garnish

SUSIE'S TIPS

■ *You can also make this recipe with trout fillets.*
■ *You could cook the tuna fillets on a barbecue, but oil it well first or it will stick.*

– Method –

■ Place the tuna steaks in a non-metallic dish, rub on the lime and chilli, and leave to marinate for at least 10 minutes.

Meanwhile, bring a large pan of well-salted water to the boil and cook the potatoes for 10 minutes or until a knife passes easily through them. Add the green beans and cook for a minute before adding the cauliflower. Cook for no more than 3–4 minutes, until the cauliflower is just tender, then drain all the vegetables.

Whilst the vegetables are cooking, start the dressing. Toast the hazelnuts in a dry pan until golden, then roughly chop. Whisk together the lemon juice and olive oil, season with salt and pepper, and add the hazelnuts. Toss some of the dressing onto the cooked vegetables to absorb the flavours.

Heat a heavy pan over a high heat; if using a griddle pan, oil it well. Flash fry the tuna steaks for 3–4 minutes each side, or to your taste, and season with salt and pepper. I like it to be a little pink in the middle. Arrange the vegetables, tomatoes and olives onto four plates, place the tuna on top and spoon some of the remaining dressing over the fish and warm salad. Garnish with lemon or lime wedges and serve warm.

MAIN COURSES: FISH

Roast Fillet of Sea Bass
with Ginger and Spring Onions

If you have ever ordered this in a Chinese restaurant you will know how expensive it can be, yet making it at home is so easy to do. The flavours are fresh, uncomplicated and utterly delicious.

SERVES 4 ■ PREPARATION TIME 10 MINUTES ■ COOKING TIME 20–25 MINUTES

– Ingredients –

*4 x 175–200g / 6–7oz sea bass fillets or other
    firm fleshed white fish, skinned*

2.5cm / 1 inch fresh ginger root, grated

4 spring onions, sliced

25g / 1oz butter, diced

1 red chilli, de-seeded and finely chopped

4 tbsp soy sauce

– Method –

■ Pre-heat the oven to 220°C / 425°F / gas mark 7.

Place the fillets on a large sheet of foil on a baking tray. Divide the remaining ingredients by four and use to season the fish. Wrap the foil loosely to seal in the flavours. Roast for 20–25 minutes. Lift the fish out of the foil and serve with the juices poured on top of the fish.

SUSIE'S TIPS

■ *You can use other firm white fleshed fish in this recipe, such as cod, haddock or halibut.*

Salmon en Croûte with Prawn Filling

*T*his delicious combination of salmon and puff pastry has an additional prawn and fresh herb filling. It looks really pretty and is perfect for entertaining on a warm summer evening.

SERVES 4 ■ PREPARATION TIME 20–25 MINUTES ■ COOKING TIME 35 MINUTES

– Ingredients –

2 x 650g / 1lb 7oz boned and skinned salmon
    fillets of the same size and thickness
    (tails are best)
juice of a lemon
salt and pepper
225g / 8oz cooked peeled prawns
20g / ¾ oz fresh chopped herbs, such as basil
    and parsley, combined
grated rind of a lemon
1 egg yolk
375g / 13oz ready-rolled puff pastry
1 egg, well beaten with a pinch of salt
    to glaze

– Method –

■ Pre-heat the oven to 200°C / 400°F / gas mark 6.

Check the salmon for bones and remove any with tweezers. Season with lemon juice, salt and pepper.

Blend two-thirds of the prawns with the herbs, lemon rind and egg yolk, and season with salt and pepper. If you do not have a food processor, then mash the prawns to a paste as best you can. Roughly chop the remaining prawns and stir into the prawn paste. Sandwich the salmon fillets together with the prawn filling.

Place the salmon on top of the rolled pastry and wrap the pastry around the fish. If you are rolling out your own pastry, roll it so that it is two and a half to three times wider than the salmon. Seal the edges with some of the beaten egg and press the edges closed with a fork. Make a couple of air slits with a sharp knife. Use any remaining pastry to decorate and brush the pastry with more beaten egg.

Bake for 35 minutes, until the pastry is golden.

Serve with new potatoes and a green vegetable or salad.

MAIN COURSES: FISH

Fish and Scallop Couscous
with Harissa and Fried Pitta

— Ingredients —

300g / 10oz couscous

40g / 1½ oz sultanas

salt and pepper

500ml / 18fl oz hot vegetable stock or water

2 tbsp olive oil

1 onion, chopped

2 cloves garlic, chopped

1 large carrot, sliced

175g / 6oz aubergine, diced

1 red pepper, quartered and sliced

115g / 4oz green beans, topped and tailed

1 tsp ground cumin

1 tsp ground cinnamon

½ tsp turmeric

½ tsp salt

600ml / 1 pint vegetable or fish stock

350g / 12oz boneless, skinless white fish,
      cut into bite-sized pieces

225g / 8oz Queen scallops

1 pitta bread

25g / 1oz butter

fresh chopped coriander leaves to garnish

FOR THE HARISSA:

1 clove garlic

½ tsp salt

½ tsp ground cumin

½ tsp coriander seeds

1 tsp chilli sauce

1 tsp tomato purée

4 tbsp olive oil

This is a great dish for entertaining as with the couscous, vegetables and fish, plus a richly flavoured broth, it is a meal in itself. If you want to add a fiery kick, serve it with the harissa sauce - but warn people that it is very hot. You need to use firm white fish for this recipe such as hake, cod or monkfish. I have used Queen scallops. These are the small offcuts of larger scallops and are not particularly expensive, but are sweet and delicious.

SERVES 4 ■ PREPARATION TIME 25 MINUTES ■ COOKING TIME 35–40 MINUTES

— Method —

■ Put the couscous into a large bowl, add the sultanas, season with salt and pepper, and mix. Add the 500ml / 18fl oz of hot vegetable stock or water, cover with cling film, and leave to absorb the liquid.

Heat the oil in a large pan and gently fry the onion until soft, then add the garlic, carrot, aubergine and red pepper, and fry for 10 minutes until the aubergine starts to soften. Cut the beans into short lengths and add along with the cumin, cinnamon, turmeric and salt. Cook for a minute or so to allow the spices to fry in the oil before adding the 600ml / 1 pint of vegetable or fish stock. Cover and cook on a high heat for 8–10 minutes, stirring from time to time.

Add the fish and scallops, and bed them down into the sauce. Cover and cook gently for 10 minutes until the fish is cooked through but not falling apart. The dish is now ready to serve, but a little fried pitta makes a nice addition. Simply break the pitta into small pieces and fry in butter until golden.

To make the harissa, slice the garlic and crush in a mortar and pestle with the salt and spices, then add the chilli sauce, tomato purée and oil.

To serve, spoon some couscous onto each plate and make a dip in the middle. Place the fish, and vegetables on top and spoon over some of the broth. Scatter over some fried pitta, along with some chopped coriander. Pass the harissa separately and let each person drizzle a little over the dish.

MAIN COURSES: FISH

Fish Cakes with Salsa

*T*hese fish cakes are light and fresh tasting compared with the traditional smoked fish and mashed potato version. They are perfect for a summer lunch or supper, and are good served hot, warm or even cold. The salsa is best made with really sweet tomatoes such as cherry tomatoes on the vine or my favourites, baby plum tomatoes.

MAKES 8 LARGE FISH CAKES ■ SERVES 4 ■ PREPARATION TIME 30 MINUTES ■ COOKING TIME 30 MINUTES

— Ingredients —

1 tbsp sunflower oil

1 onion, chopped

3 tbsp water

1 tsp sugar

55g / 2oz white bread

a little milk to soak the bread

225g / 8oz haddock and coley fillets, skinned

1 tsp creamed or grated horseradish

1 small handful parsley, chopped

1 egg white

salt and pepper

2 tbsp plain flour seasoned with paprika

oil for frying

FOR THE SALSA:

225g / 8oz cherry or baby plum tomatoes, cut into small dice

1 small red onion, very finely chopped

1–2 red chillies, de-seeded and very finely chopped

a good handful of coriander leaves, roughly chopped

juice of 1 lime or ½ large lemon to taste

salt and pepper

SUSIE'S TIPS

■ *Try making mini-sized fish cakes and serve cold along with the salsa as a nibble.*

— Method —

■ Heat the oil in a saucepan and add the onion. Fry over a gentle heat until translucent, then add the water and sugar, and cook for 10 minutes until the onions are really soft.

Meanwhile, soak the bread in a little milk for a couple of minutes (you could use water if you prefer) and squeeze out all the excess liquid.

Check the fish fillets for bones. If you have a food processor, cube the fish and process along with the onions, bread, horseradish, parsley and egg white, and season with salt and pepper. Otherwise mince or finely chop the fish and combine the ingredients together.

With floured hands, shape the fish into balls and flatten into patties, coating each in seasoned flour. Heat the oil in a large frying pan and cook gently for 18–20 minutes, turning halfway through.

To make the salsa, combine all the ingredients together and season to taste. The amount of lime or lemon juice you add will depend on the heat of the chillies. Try to find a balance between the sweetness of the tomatoes, heat of the chillies and zing of the citrus fruit.

MAIN COURSES: FISH

Vegetarian and Vegetables

Left: Green Beans with Bacon and Peppers, Warm Tomatoes with Boursin, and Broad Bean and Mint Mash

Courgette and Mushroom Pasta

*T*his is a simple pasta recipe that is both quick and easy to make. The combination of courgettes, mushrooms, sun-dried tomatoes, thyme and Parmesan go very well together. Any short pasta shape can be used.

SERVES 4 ■ PREPARATION TIME 15 MINUTES ■ COOKING TIME 25 MINUTES

— Ingredients —

3 tbsp olive oil

1 medium onion, chopped

2 cloves garlic, chopped

600g / 1lb 5oz courgettes, sliced

salt and pepper

1 tsp fresh thyme leaves, chopped

250g / 9oz chestnut mushrooms, sliced

350g / 12oz short pasta shapes

8–10 sun-dried tomatoes in oil, chopped

plenty of freshly grated Parmesan to garnish

— Method —

■ Heat the oil in a large frying pan and add the onions. Fry until soft, then add the garlic and courgettes and fry over a medium to high heat. Season well with salt and pepper, and add the thyme. When the courgettes are golden in colour, add the mushrooms and cook until they are soft.

Meanwhile cook the pasta in a pan of boiling salted water until al dente, drain well and combine with the courgette mixture. Stir in the sun-dried tomatoes and serve with grated Parmesan.

FERN'S TIPS

■ *If you like strong flavours, stir in some chopped black olives and capers with the sun-dried tomatoes.*

Flour Tortillas
with Guacamole and Sour Cream

*T*his is a very quick and simple dish that is great for informal eating as you eat the tortillas with your fingers. Each person fills the tortilla themselves and spoons on sour cream and guacamole. Either use my recipe for guacamole or buy your own, in which case you will want to sprinkle coriander leaves onto the tortilla as well.

SERVES 4 ■ PREPARATION TIME 10 MINUTES ■ COOKING TIME 10 MINUTES

– Ingredients –

1 tbsp chilli flavoured oil or other

1 red, yellow and green pepper (3 in all), halved and sliced into thin batons

1 Spanish-style onion, halved and sliced

2 medium courgettes, cut into thin batons like the peppers

salt and pepper

8 flour tortillas

TO GARNISH:

150ml / 5fl oz sour cream

guacamole from recipe given on page 75, or shop bought, plus a handful of fresh coriander leaves

– Method –

■ Heat the oil in a wok and, when hot, add all the vegetables. Season with salt and pepper and stir fry for 8–10 minutes until the vegetables soften.

Warm the tortillas in a low oven or in a microwave according to the instructions on the packet. Bring the tortillas to the table wrapped in a clean tea towel to help keep them warm.

To serve: spoon some of the vegetable mixture into the middle of a tortilla, spoon on a little sour cream and guacamole, and a few coriander leaves if you want. Fold up one end of the tortilla and then roll over the sides, encasing the filling. Eat with your fingers and try to avoid the sour cream oozing down your shirt as you bite into it.

FERN'S TIPS

■ *You can add strips of chicken, lamb or beef to the stir fry if you want a meaty alternative.*

Spinach and Feta Pancake Stack

*T*his is a substantial vegetarian dish. These pancakes are light in texture but thicker in the American style and the batter is flavoured with spinach and feta cheese. The pancakes are then layered with a rich tomato and mushroom sauce.

SERVES 4 ■ PREPARATION TIME 25–30 MINUTES ■ COOKING TIME 35 MINUTES

– Ingredients –

FOR THE BATTER:

225g / 8oz frozen leaf spinach

2 eggs, separated

115g / 4oz plain flour

225ml / 8fl oz milk

225g / 8oz feta cheese, crumbled

1/2 tsp ground nutmeg

pepper

15g / 1/2 oz butter

FOR THE TOMATO SAUCE:

1 tbsp olive oil

1 onion, finely chopped

400g/14oz tin chopped tomatoes

50ml/2fl oz red wine

1 tbsp tomato purée

1/4 tsp dried thyme

1/4 tsp dried oregano

salt and pepper

For the mushrooms:

1 tbsp oil

300g / 10 1/2 oz flat field mushrooms,
        sliced 5mm / 1/4 inch thick

salt and pepper

juice of 1/2 a lemon

sprigs of thyme to garnish

– Method –

■ Defrost the spinach – this can be done by heating it in a saucepan for a couple of minutes. Drain well, squeezing out as much of the water as you possibly can so that the spinach is almost 'dry', then roughly chop.

Make the pancake batter by adding the egg yolks to the flour, then beat together, incorporating the milk a little at a time until you have a smooth batter. Whisk the egg whites until stiff and use a metal spoon to fold them into the batter, along with the chopped spinach, three-quarters of the feta, the nutmeg and some pepper.

Add a knob of butter to a frying pan and make the pancakes, adding a little more butter when needed. Cook the pancakes for 3 minutes each side over a gentle heat and when they are ready to be turned over, dimples will appear on the surface of the batter – keep warm whilst you make more. You should make eight pancakes in all. They will keep well in the bottom of a low oven while you prepare the sauce and mushrooms.

To make the Tomato sauce: Heat the oil in a saucepan and fry the onion until soft, then add the rest of the ingredients and simmer for 10 minutes. If you like a smooth sauce, blend it at this stage otherwise leave it as it is.

To cook the Mushrooms: heat the oil in a frying pan and briefly fry the mushrooms over a high heat, season with salt and pepper and a generous squeeze of lemon juice.

To serve: put one pancake onto each plate, spoon on a little of the sauce and some of the mushrooms, top with another pancake and more mushrooms. Dot some of the remaining feta on top. Spoon the rich tomato sauce around the base of each pancake stack and garnish with a sprig of fresh thyme.

Summer Dauphinoise

*D*auphinoise is typical of good French bistro cooking. Layers of potato are delicately flavoured with garlic and cream, and cooked until meltingly soft. I can think of nothing better to eat them with than a good steak and green salad. It is also a very well behaved dish that you can keep warm for up to an hour.

SERVES 4-6 ■ PREPARATION TIME 25 MINUTES ■ COOKING TIME APPROX 1 HOUR

– Ingredients –

650g / 1lb 7oz potatoes, peeled
40g / 1½ oz butter
1 large clove garlic, thinly sliced
salt and pepper
freshly grated nutmeg
2 tbsp chopped chives
200ml / 7fl oz half fat crème fraîche
100ml / 3½ fl oz milk
55g / 2oz Gruyère, finely grated

– Method –

■ Pre-heat the oven to 180°C / 350°F / gas mark 4. (You can cook the potatoes on a lower heat if you have something else in the oven, just adjust the cooking time accordingly.)

The secret of a good dauphinoise is to slice the potatoes as thinly as you can. Purists say you should be able to read a newspaper through them, but that is too far-fetched. Chefs would use a mandolin, but you or I could use a wide potato peeler, a food processor with a fine slicing blade or a good old fashioned razor-sharp knife. Slice the potatoes into a bowl of cold water.

Grease a 1.2 litre / 2 pint ovenproof dish with 15g / ½ oz of the butter. Layer the slices of potato so that they overlap on the bottom of the dish. Dot with a little butter, a little garlic, season well with salt and pepper and a little grated nutmeg, and scatter on some of the chives. Repeat the process until you have used up all the potato.

Mix together the crème fraîche and milk, and pour over the dish, nudging the liquid down the sides of the dish as well. Sprinkle the cheese over the top and bake for 1 hour or until the potatoes are soft and the top is golden. Allow the potatoes to 'set' for 10 minutes before serving.

Warm Tomatoes with Boursin

PHOTOGRAPH ON PAGE 104

*T*his is one of those marriages made in heaven. It works well as a side dish to grilled meat or fish but, boy, is it good with just a hunk of warm soft bread and a bottle of wine

SERVES 4 ■ PREPARATION TIME 5 MINUTES ■ COOKING TIME 15 MINUTES

– Ingredients –

8 medium vine ripened tomatoes, fairly
    thickly sliced
½ (just under 80g / 3oz) Boursin cheese
2 tbsp olive oil
salt and pepper

– Method –

■ Pre-heat the oven to 180°C / 350°F / gas mark 4.
    Arrange the tomatoes in an ovenproof dish, dot with the Boursin and drizzle over the olive oil. Season and bake for 15 minutes. The cheese will have melted and the tomatoes will have sweetened in the oven.

Roasted Aubergines and Tomatoes

*T*his is a really good vegetable side dish as it acts like a chunky sauce to enliven plainly cooked fish or meat.

SERVES 4 ■ PREPARATION TIME 10 MINUTES ■ COOKING TIME 40 MINUTES

– Ingredients –

1 large aubergine, cut into 1cm / ½ inch
    cubes
2 large beef tomatoes, cubed to the same size
1 large clove of garlic, squashed but left
    whole
2–3 tbsp olive oil
a small pinch of dried thyme
salt and pepper

– Method –

■ Pre-heat the oven to 190°C / 375°F / gas mark 5.
    Place all the ingredients in an ovenproof dish and stir to coat the vegetables in the oil. Roast for 40 minutes. Stir once again and serve.

Green Beans with Bacon and Peppers

P H O T O G R A P H   O N   P A G E   1 0 4

I often like to serve vegetables plain, but it does get a bit boring. These green beans would go very well with a roast or chops and when I made them, I sat down and ate a bowlful for lunch with bread and a chunk of cheese. How sublime vegetables can be. These are good eaten hot or cold.

SERVES 4 ■ PREPARATION TIME 10 MINUTES ■ COOKING TIME 15 MINUTES

– Ingredients –

300g / 10½ oz fine green beans,
    topped and tailed
1–2 tbsp olive oil
4 rashers rindless streaky bacon or
    70g / 2½ oz cubed pancetta
½ each of onion, green and red pepper,
    very thinly sliced
salt and pepper

– Method –

■ Bring a pan of salted water to the boil, add the beans and cook for approximately 8–10 minutes until tender, then drain.

    Meanwhile heat the oil in a wok or large frying pan, add the bacon and fry until golden. Depending on the amount of fat that comes off the bacon, you may want to tip a little out. Turn down the heat, add the rest of the ingredients, season and stir fry gently for 5 minutes. Add the drained beans, mix and serve.

Broad Bean and Mint Mash

P H O T O G R A P H   O N   P A G E   1 0 4

This is a good thick, bright green purée that Susie's husband has called 'posh mushy peas.' If you are lucky enough to grow broad beans, use fresh, otherwise a packet of frozen will do. It goes particularly well with pork or white fish dishes.

SERVES 4–6 ■ PREPARATION TIME 5 MINUTES ■ COOKING TIME 15 MINUTES

– Ingredients –

650g / 1lb 7oz fresh broad beans
8 mint leaves
4 tbsp Greek yoghurt
25g / 1oz butter, optional
1 tsp Dijon mustard
salt and pepper

– Method –

■ Boil the beans in a pan of salted water for 10–12 minutes until tender. Add the mint leaves to the pot for the last minute of cooking to soften them. Drain and place the beans and mint in a food processor along with all the other ingredients and blend until almost smooth. If you do not have a food processor, you could mash the beans, chop the mint and mix the ingredients together for a rougher purée that will still taste delicious.

VEGETARIAN AND VEGETABLES

Petit Pois à la Française

This dish is a real surprise as it combines cooked lettuce, peas and mint. You may think the idea of cooking lettuce an odd one, but we readily tuck into raw and cooked spinach. The recipe transforms a packet of frozen peas into a really good dish that is the perfect partner to grilled, roast or barbecued meat or fish. Of course, if you are lucky enough to have plenty of fresh peas, use them, but you may need to cook them a little longer.

SERVES 4 ■ PREPARATION TIME 8 MINUTES ■ COOKING TIME 35 MINUTES

– Ingredients –

25g / 1oz butter
1 small onion or ½ a large onion, chopped
2 little gem lettuces, sliced
280g / 10oz frozen peas
3–4 fresh mint leaves
150ml / ¼ pint hot water
salt and pepper
15g / ½ oz plain flour

– Method –

■ Pre-heat the oven to 180°C / 350°F / gas mark 4.

Melt half the butter in a small heatproof casserole (if you do not have one, or a saucepan that can go into the oven, then fry the onions and transfer them to an ovenproof dish covered with foil). Soften the onions in the butter, take off the heat and stir in the lettuce, peas, mint and water. Season well with salt and pepper, cover, and transfer to the oven.

Cook for 15 minutes, then mix the remaining butter and the flour together to make a paste. Add the paste to the peas and stir until it dissolves. Replace the lid and return the casserole to the oven to cook for a further 15 minutes. The butter and flour will thicken the dish.

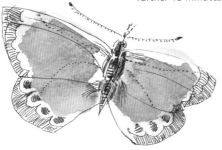

Picnics and Sandwiches

A spontaneous trip to the beach or countryside on a beautiful summer's day is what memories are made of. All too often I hear myself say 'Oh, I'll just throw together a picnic'. This turns out to be quite a stressful experience, buttering endless slices of bread, scraping out empty jars of peanut butter and rifling through the fridge for the odd slice of ham or chunk of cucumber. Of course, if one could only count on the weather and plan a picnic, things would be different. I would cook sausages, chicken legs and hard-boil eggs the night before.

Here are some ideas on how to make a last-minute picnic easier to prepare and more interesting to eat. Buy a French stick – you may already keep part-baked ones in the freezer. Split the loaf in half lengthways and remove a little of the bread from one side to make way for the filling. Butter one side and put mayonnaise on the other, now fill with your favourite fillings. You may prefer to fill one end for the children and one for grown-ups. Wrap the loaf in cling film and take a bread knife with you. Simply slice the loaf into when you get there.

Here is Susie's all-time favourite sandwich filling, tuna mayonnaise and some other suggestions.

Tuna Mayonnaise

■ FILLS 1 BAGUETTE OR 4 SANDWICHES ■

– Ingredients –

200g / 7oz tinned tuna fish chunks

25g / 1oz celery, finely chopped

25g / 1oz red pepper, very finely diced

25g / 1oz cucumber, very finely diced

12 capers, roughly chopped

8 pitted black olives, roughly chopped

a good splash of Worcestershire sauce

2 tsp freshly squeezed lemon juice

salt and pepper

4–6 tbsp mayonnaise, how much you add
        will depend on taste

iceberg lettuce, shredded

– Method –

■ Mix all the ingredients together well. Spread onto the bread, and cover with the lettuce. You can make the filling in advance and leave it covered in the fridge overnight.

OTHER FILLING SUGGESTIONS AND TIPS:

The key ingredient to making a good sandwich is good fresh bread. Look out for unusual breads, such as bagels, rye bread, ciabatta rolls and pitta bread. If using pitta bread, the round kind sometimes called pitta pockets work best for sandwiches. Just make a small opening in one side and stuff them. It is easier to open them if they are warm. Spread mayonnaise (not salad cream) onto one side of the bread and butter on the other. If using meat I like to spread the buttered side with a mild mustard. Do not be tempted to overfill the sandwich or it will be messy to eat. Lastly, tomatoes and other 'wet' vegetables are only suitable if the sandwich is to be eaten fairly quickly or the bread will turn soggy.

Susie's Sandwiches

Sandwich One

slices of Emmental cheese

salami

slices of tomato

mixed salad leaves

salt and pepper

a good spread of Dijon mustard
        on the buttered side

Sandwich Two

smoked salmon or trout

cream cheese

lemon juice

black pepper

slices of cucumber

shredded iceberg lettuce

Sandwich Three

chèvre or other goat's cheese

roasted red peppers (you can buy these
        in jars covered in olive oil)

a few capers

mixed salad leaves (including rocket)

salt and pepper

Perfect Picnics

The following recipes from the book would be lovely on a grander picnic, if you run to plates and forks on such occasions.

Puddings and Baking

Left: Hazelnut Torte with Raspberry and Cream Filling

Go Wild Chocolate Flan

I love recipes like this. Zero cooking required! It's the equivalent of a flat-packed bookcase, only simpler! All credit goes to Susie's Danish friend for this idea. She made a pink one for her daughter's birthday using strawberries, cream, marshmallows, pink icing, white chocolate and hundreds and thousands. This is an adult's version with alcohol and bitter chocolate. It calls for three, small, ready-made supermarket flan cases (or two large ones), stacked on top of each other to make a very tall cake. Go to town with the fillings, adding your family's favourite fruits and toppings.

SERVES 6–8 FOR A SMALL CAKE ■ PREPARATION TIME 15 MINUTES

– Ingredients –

3 flan cases approx. 19cm / 7½ inches in diameter

50ml / 2fl oz brandy, sherry or fruit juice

200ml / ⅓ pint whipping cream, whipped

200ml / ⅓ pint bought fresh cream custard

125g / 4½ oz raspberries, you can used tinned or frozen if you like

100g / 3½ oz dark chocolate (50% cocoa solids)

125g / 4½ oz strawberries, sliced

strawberry or raspberry sorbet to garnish

– Method –

Splash the brandy, sherry or fruit juice over two of the flans. Mix three-quarters of the cream with the custard, gently squash the raspberries and add them to the mixture. Chop 20g / ¾ oz of the chocolate and add this too. Pile half the raspberry cream onto an alcohol-soaked flan. Top with the other soaked flan, pile on the rest of the cream and top that with the third flan.

Melt the remaining chocolate in a small bowl over a pan of simmering water. Pour this on top of the third flan and let the chocolate dribble over the sides of the cake. When the chocolate is set, spread the remaining plain cream on top. Decorate with the sliced strawberries. Put into the fridge for 20 minutes to allow the chocolate to set hard.

Before serving, spoon some of the sorbet on top of the cake to finish it off or, if you feel this is a little over the top, then serve the sorbet alongside.

Scones

The secret of making good scones is gentle handling. Overhandling will result in tough, biscuit-like scones. They do not take long to make and are best eaten warm, split in half and filled with clotted cream and strawberry jam. I'm a bit pedantic about which goes on first! Spread the cream on (like butter) and then the jam. If you've got fresh strawberries, slice them and use instead of the jam. I am also fond of wholemeal scones served warm with butter and honey.

SERVES 4 ■ PREPARATION TIME 15 MINUTES ■ COOKING TIME 12–15 MINUTES

– Ingredients –

225g / 8oz self-raising flour
1 tsp baking powder
55g / 2oz butter or margarine, cold
25g / 1oz caster sugar
7 tbsp milk, plus extra to glaze

FERN'S TIPS

■ *If you want to make wholemeal scones use half wholemeal and half self-raising flour.*
■ *For fruit scones, add 55g / 2oz of sultanas, raisins, candied peel or dried dates.*

– Method –

■ Pre-heat the oven to 220°C / 425°F / gas mark 7.

Sift the flour and baking powder together into a bowl. Cut the butter or margarine into cubes and rub into the flour with your fingertips, incorporating as much air as possible. Add the milk a little at a time, mixing and cutting through the mixture with a blunt knife. Turn out onto a lightly floured surface and gently knead the mixture together. Roll out to 1cm / ½ inch thick and cut into rounds. Place on a greased baking sheet and brush each scone with a little milk. Bake for 12–15 minutes until the scones are pale gold.

Hazelnut Torte
with Raspberry and Cream Filling

PHOTOGRAPH ON PAGE 116

This is light, moist sponge cake that is made with no fat, until you fill it that is. I like to use a fresh cream and raspberry filling, but a chocolate or mocha butter icing would also be good. If you like plain cakes then dust it with icing sugar and eat it as it is. It is a generous sized cake that would easily serve 10 people.

SERVES 10 ■ PREPARATION TIME: 15–20 MINUTES USING AN ELECTRIC WHISK, PLUS 5 MINUTES FOR FILLING
COOKING TIME 50 MINUTES

– Ingredients –

FOR THE TORTE:

225g / 8oz shelled hazelnuts
    (with or without their brown skin)
9 eggs
200g / 7oz caster sugar
2 tbsp brandy
115g / 4oz self-raising flour
you will also need a greased 23cm / 9 inch
    spring form cake tin

FOR THE FILLING:

300ml / 10fl oz double cream
2 tbsp icing sugar, plus extra for dusting
½ tsp vanilla essence
225g / 8oz fresh raspberries
extra cream, raspberries and hazelnuts to
    decorate, optional

FERN'S TIPS

■ *A quick decoration for the top of a sponge can be made by putting a doily on top of a cake, dusting the icing sugar over it and removing the doily, to leave a lacy pattern.*

– Method –

■ Pre-heat the oven to 180°C / 350°F / gas mark 4.

Roast the whole hazelnuts in the oven for 10–15 minutes, but watch that they do not burn. Cool a little and then either chop in a food processor until they become like breadcrumbs, or chop as finely as you can by hand.

Separate the eggs. When working, as here, with a large number of eggs it is best to crack each one separately over a small bowl in case an egg yolk breaks and ruins the whites. Beat the egg yolks until creamy with an electric hand whisk if you have one, then add the sugar and brandy and whisk until pale and mousse-like.

Mix the hazelnuts and flour together. Carefully wash and dry your whisk and whisk the egg whites until stiff. Add alternate spoonfuls of egg white and nut mixture to the egg yolk mixture, carefully folding in each addition with a large metal spoon. Work gently so as to keep in as much air as you can. Pour into the cake tin and bake in the middle of the oven for 50 minutes.

Leave to cool in the tin before turning out. If you wish to fill the torte, slice through the middle with a bread knife. If you can, slice it into three layers.

To make the filling, whip the cream, sugar and vanilla together until thick but not grainy. Spread over the layers of the cake, scatter over the raspberries and sandwich the layers together. Dust with icing sugar.

Yoghurt and Orange Semolina Cake

T his is an extremely yummy and versatile cake that would make just as good a pudding served with crème fraîche as it would a tea time cake. It is also good the following day so, if you're entertaining, you can get ahead. Don't let the memories of school semolina put you off. The semolina serves only to lend a nutty almost grainy texture, and the whole thing is drenched in a citrus syrup flavoured with orange flower water. Heaven.

SERVES 6–8 ■ PREPARATION TIME 15–20 MINUTES ■ COOKING TIME 55–60 MINUTES

– Ingredients –

55g / 2oz unsalted butter, softened

175g / 6oz caster sugar

3 medium eggs

250ml / 9fl oz plain yoghurt

grated rind of 1 orange and 1 lemon

175g / 6oz semolina

55g / 2oz plain flour

55g / 2oz ground almonds

1 level tsp baking powder

pinch of salt

FOR THE SYRUP:

115g / 4oz granulated sugar

juice of an orange

juice of ½ a lemon

1 tsp orange flower water, optional

– Method –

■ Pre-heat the oven to 180°C / 350°F / gas mark 4.

Cream the butter and sugar together until pale and fluffy. You can use an electric whisk or food processor if you prefer. Add the eggs one at a time, adding a little of the flour if the mixture curdles. Add the yoghurt and orange and lemon rind.

Add the remaining ingredients and mix well.

Grease and line a 20cm / 8 inch loose-bottomed cake tin that is at least 2.5cm / 1 inch deep. Fill with the cake mixture and bake in the middle of the oven for 30 minutes. After this time cover the cake tin with foil and return to the oven for a further 25–30 minutes. Test that the cake is cooked by inserting a skewer into it. If ready, it will come out clean.

Meanwhile make the syrup by slowly heating all the ingredients (except the orange flower water) in a small saucepan. Once the sugar has dissolved, bring to the boil and boil rapidly for 4–6 minutes until the liquid becomes syrupy, then add the orange flower water.

Turn out the cake onto a large plate whilst still hot and pierce the top all over with a skewer. Pour over the syrup and allow the cake to cool and soak up the syrup before serving.

This is a moist cake best eaten with a fork rather than with fingers.

Summer Fruit Terrine

*T*errines are usually savoury and look a bit like pâté until you slice them. Then you see – rather as in a stick of rock – layers of meat set in jelly. How much more beautiful it would look if the centre was fruit set in sweet jelly? Some time ago, Susie bought a beautiful summer fruit terrine from a very expensive shop in Knightsbridge. She wanted to have a special pudding to take to an elegant picnic but did not have much time to make one. The idea she came up with was like a summer pudding, but it sliced beautifully. She has since worked on the idea and come up with a quick and easy recipe, using one of our favourite shortcut ingredients – a bag of frozen summer fruits – which are set in jelly and easy to transport, should you wish to take them on a picnic.

SERVES 6 ■ PREPARATION TIME 15 MINUTES ■ REQUIRES 3 HOURS TO SET IN THE FRIDGE

– Ingredients –

500g / 1lb 2oz frozen summer fruits
2 tbsp caster sugar
7–8 medium thick slices white bread
1 sachet of raspberry jelly, to make
    600ml / 1 pint
fresh raspberries, strawberries and
    blueberries to decorate
icing sugar to dust

– Method –

■ Defrost the fruits, reserving all the juice that comes out of them, and stir in the sugar. Put the defrosted fruits in a sieve and catch every last drop of their juice too, and put in a shallow dish.

Cut the crusts off the bread, dip two slices into the juice and use to line the base of a 450g / 1lb loaf tin. Cut three slices in half, dip them in juice and line the sides of the tin. Fill with the fruits. Make up the jelly so that it is liquid and pour it over the fruits until it comes to the top of the bread. Dip the last of the bread into the fruit juice and cover. Use extra bread to fill any gaps. Pour over any remaining fruit juice and a little more of the jelly so that the sides and the top are just covered with jelly. Set in the fridge for at least 2 hours before turning out onto a serving dish. If you wish to transport the terrine, do so at this stage in the tin.

Decorate with fresh fruit and dust with icing sugar before serving in slices with double cream or sweetened crème fraîche.

FERN'S TIPS

■ *You can make your own jelly from your favourite fresh juice and gelatine, or its vegetarian alternative.*

Arranged Fruit Platter

*I*f you don't want to have a fattening pudding but prefer fruit at the end of meal it is so much nicer to serve it prepared rather than plonking a fruit bowl down on the table. It also allows you to demonstrate your artistic flair.

I like to have a selection of fruits, choosing them for sweetness, flavour and colour. Favourites are strawberries, small bunches of grapes, slices of orange, cantaloupe or watermelon and physallis with their paper husks folded back to reveal their bright orange fruits. Also fresh figs, cherries and loganberries, lychees and mango, alongside fresh dates or dried medjool dates. The important thing is to be generous, and to offer a cornucopia of ripe, delicious fruit.

Decorate the platter with vine leaves and edible flowers, and dot chocolates wrapped in foil or topped with crystallized violets among the fruit.

You can arrange the platter in advance and keep it, covered, in the fridge, but do let the fruits return to room temperature before serving or much of their flavour will be lost.

Summer Fruit Mousse

*T*his is the true taste of summer. You can use a mixture of whichever berries you fancy – strawberries, raspberries, blueberries or loganberries. If you prefer, you can use a packet of frozen summer fruits (these have become a staple in my freezer).

SERVES 6 ■ PREPARATION TIME 15 MINUTES ■ REQUIRES 2 HOURS TO SET IN THE FRIDGE

– Ingredients –

450g / 1lb summer berries, defrosted if frozen

85g / 3oz caster sugar

1 sachet (70g / 2½ oz) gelatine

300ml / ½ pint double cream

200g / 7oz Greek yoghurt

whole berries and bunches of currants
     to decorate

– Method –

■ Purée the berries and mix with the sugar. Make up the gelatine according to the instructions on the packet. Whip the cream until fairly stiff but not grainy and mix with the yoghurt.

Stir the gelatine into the fruit and fold in the cream. Pour into a pretty dish and refrigerate for at least 2 hours before serving to allow the gelatine to set. Decorate with berries and currants.

Ricotta, Orange and Chocolate Tart

— Ingredients —

250g / 9oz ricotta

grated rind of an orange

85g / 3oz chopped glacé fruits or candied peel

40g / 1½ oz dark chocolate
    (50% cocoa solids), chopped like
    chocolate drops

1 egg and 1 egg yolk, beaten

55g / 2oz caster sugar

a few drops vanilla essence

1 x 20cm / 8 inch ready-made
    sweet pastry case

*S*usie discovered the joys of the supermarket ready-made sweet pastry case last year when she invented the incredibly successful Baked Chocolate Tart and Lemon Cheesecake. (See a copy of Fern's Family Favourites for those recipes!) This time we have gone for the classic combination of orange and chocolate. It's a very rich tart, delicious served with good strong coffee at the end of a meal or at tea time. And please feel free to lie about the pastry case. Of course you made it yourself.

SERVES 6 ■ PREPARATION TIME 12 MINUTES
COOKING TIME 30 MINUTES

— Method —

■ Pre-heat the oven to 190°C / 375°F / gas mark 5.
   Simply mix all the filling ingredients together and pour into the pastry case. Smooth the surface and bake for 30 minutes. Serve warm.

Jazzed-up Ice Cream
Butterscotch, Chocolate Fudge and Raspberry Sauces

A dark chocolate, butterscotch or fresh raspberry sauce poured over ice cream makes a good last-minute pudding. The chocolate and butterscotch becomes fudge-like over the cold ice cream. Add halved and cored poached pears and you upgrade it to a quite special pudding. Best of all, the sauces can be made ahead of time and kept in the fridge for up to a week. Reheat the chocolate and butterscotch before serving.

You could also try pouring the raspberry sauce over the Summer Fruit Mousse, Summer Fruit Terrine and the Hazelnut torte (see pages 124, 123 and 120).

Butterscotch Sauce

– Ingredients –

85g / 3oz unsalted butter
200g / 7oz caster or soft brown sugar
2 tbsp golden syrup
100ml / 3½ fl oz double cream
a few drops of vanilla essence

– Method –

■ Melt the butter in a saucepan over a gentle heat, add the sugar and syrup, and stir until the sugar has dissolved. Add the cream and bring to the boil. Take from the heat and stir in the vanilla. Serve warm or cold.

Chocolate Fudge Sauce

– Ingredients –

175ml / 6fl oz double cream
50ml / 2fl oz golden syrup
175g / 6oz caster sugar
85g / 3oz dark bitter chocolate (50% cocoa
        solids), broken into squares
25g / 1oz butter
1 tsp vanilla essence

– Method –

■ Heat the cream, syrup and sugar in a small pan until the sugar is dissolved. Add the chocolate and stir until melted and thick (this can take up to 25 minutes over a low heat). Take the pan from the heat and stir in the butter and vanilla. This is best served hot.

Raspberry Sauce

FERN'S TIPS

■ *Turn this into a knickerbocker glory by filling a tall glass with a little plain cake, fresh fruit and two flavours of ice cream, then pour over the sauce and top with whipped cream and a cherry! As a child I would stand on a chair with my arm elbow-deep in the glass trying to scrape out every last bit.*

– Ingredients –

225g / 8oz raspberries, defrosted if frozen
55g / 2oz icing sugar
1 tbsp crème de cassis or Kirsch (optional)

– Method –

■ Purée the raspberries in a food processor with the sugar, then taste and add more sugar if necessary. Pass through a sieve to remove the raspberry seeds. Stir the crème de cassis or Kirsch into the purée. Serve chilled.

Index

Page numbers in bold type are where you'll find recipes, and in italic type where you'll find sumptuous full-page photographs. Other entries refer to ingredients and tips.